EULOGY
OF
LAWYERS
WRITTEN BY A LAWYER

D0807425

EULOGY
OF
LAWYERS
WRITTEN BY A LAWYER

Jacob A. Stein

Preface by Bryan A. Garner

The Lawbook Exchange, Ltd.
Clark, New Jersey

ISBN-13: 978-1-58477-969-8 (cloth)
ISBN-10: 1-58477-969-1 (cloth)
ISBN-13: 978-1-58477-970-4 (paperback)
ISBN-10: 1-58477-970-5 (paperback)

THE LAWBOOK EXCHANGE, LTD.
33 Terminal Avenue
Clark, New Jersey 07066-1321

Please see our website for a selection of our other publications and fine
facsimile reprints of classic works of legal history:
www.lawbookexchange.com

Library of Congress Cataloging-in-Publication Data

Stein, Jacob A.
 Eulogy of lawyers / by Jacob A. Stein.
     p. cm.
  ISBN-13: 978-1-58477-969-8 (cloth : alk. paper)
  ISBN-10: 1-58477-969-1 (cloth : alk. paper)
  ISBN-13: 978-1-58477-970-4 (pbk. : alk. paper)
  ISBN-10: 1-58477-970-5 (pbk. : alk. paper)
  1. Stein, Jacob A. 2. Lawyers—Washington (D.C.)—Biography.
I. Title.
  KF373.S689A3 2009
  340.092—dc22
  [B]
                              2009008300

Printed in the United States of America on acid-free paper

To Mary

CONTENTS

Odds & Ends

PREFACE

I n 1981, the noted Washington law-
yer Jake Stein published a scintillating anthology of his essays, *Legal
Spectator*, in one of which he explained the origin of his fascination
with the Italian lawyer-writer Piero Calamandrei. At auction he
had purchased a lot of 18 books in the genre of legal facetiae. In
Stein's words: "The first book that came to hand when I unpacked
my treasure trove was *Eulogy for Judges*. I have now read this whimsical masterpiece over several times.... The author's purpose is to
explain to lawyers how to get along with judges."

Again, that was 1981. Twenty-six years later—having admired
Jake Stein from afar as a literary lawyer—I met him and we became
friends. Piero Calamandrei has figured in every conversation we've
had, wide-ranging though they've been. Under Stein's influence, I
too came to admire Calamandrei's whimsical masterpiece, which
not coincidentally came to be quoted favorably in a book in which
I was collaborating with Justice Antonin Scalia in 2007–2008.

Stein's own writing possesses many of the virtues of Calamandrei's: a wry sense of humor; an unvarnished, no-nonsense view of human nature; a realistic, hard-boiled understanding of the travails of litigation; a cynical view of wily, uncooperative clients; and a lucid, spartan style.

Calamandrei has influenced Stein every bit as much as Robert Jackson influenced Antonin Scalia, Vladimir Nabokov influenced Ruth Bader Ginsburg, Fred Rodell influenced Charles Alan Wright, or William F. Buckley influenced Bruce Selya. And so Jacob Stein has named the book *Eulogy of Lawyers*. The purpose of the book, as far as I can deduce it, is to explain to the world at large how to understand lawyers—from their own point of view.

Stein's essays are evocative. You must read between the lines. His essay "Truth, Falsehood, and the Law," for example, could easily descend into a predictable bathos by which the author might moralistically decry lying, call for legislative reform of the federal false-statement statute, or refute those who are cocksure about the reliability of lie detectors. But bathos not being in his writerly makeup, Stein does none of those things—explicitly. He does all of them implicitly—and pleasurably, without a soapbox.

There are dozens of examples of this sort of thing in the book. And there are dozens of passages that will delight any lawyer with a literary bent—the discovery of an Oklahoma advocate named Moman Pruiett, the reflections on John Mortimer's life, or the brilliant exposition of the art of conversation (and why lawyers excel at it).

Stein is part Calamandrei, but he is also part Lamb (think *Essays of Elia*), part Hazlitt (think *Familiar Essays*), and part Montaigne (no hyperbole there—just dip in and see). Stein is a rare breed: a superb, noted advocate—one of the finest of his day—who

is also a literary essayist. I can think of only two comparable prede-
cessors: Lord Brougham and Clarence Darrow.

Sadly, lawyers on the whole aren't a literary bunch—and most
will never open these pages to revel in the delights to be found on
virtually every page. So you've somehow been drawn to this book
and are now about to benefit from its wisdom. Count yourself
among a highly select group: the literary lawyers who value history, relish literature, enjoy a good turn of phrase, and appreciate
an apt allusion now and then. Let me detain you no more from the
whimsical masterpiece that follows.

Bryan A. Garner

INTRODUCTION

Two books prompted this book. The first was Piero Calamandrei's *Eulogy of Judges*, a remarkable commentary on judges, lawyers, clients, and the everyday practice of law, no matter where, no matter when. Calamandrei practiced law in the Italian courts in the 1920's and 1930's, and his comments are the same as if he practiced in Chicago or New York. His short ironic paragraphs mix the real and the aspirational.

I have reason to believe that Mr. Calamandrei intended to write a *Eulogy of Lawyers*, but he never got around to it. The best I can do in this book is to offer up a plagiarism focusing on lawyers the way Calamandrei focused on judges.

The second book is Reginald L. Hine's Confessions of an Un-Common Attorney. He opened his book by saying he spent 40 years dealing with his clients' affairs and the time had come for him to tidy up the overcrowded curiosity shop of thoughts, recollections, and the twists and turns of a law practice. What follows is a tidying up of my own curiosity shop.

★ ★ ★

Years ago, I envied lawyers who stood up in court and announced, with great indignation, "In my 30 years of practice, I have never heard anything like what my opponent just said to the court." Here was a dramatic closer that compelled attention and demeaned that young upstart who was citing all those cases.

As I write I am in my 60th year of practice. I think I have earned the prescriptive right to stand up and declare, "In my 60 years of practice ...," for whatever effect it may have. However, I do not plan to do so.

I was speaking with a friend who is also a member of the 60-year club. We questioned whether age denies us what it takes to read documents, court rules, fine print, and appellate opinions that run more than 10 pages. Do we still have that vigor of mind?

My friend referred me to Justice Felix Frankfurter's diary dated December 9, 1947. The Justice noted that he had just visited with Chief Justice Charles Evans Hughes. The chief, although advanced in years, impressed Justice Frankfurter with his vigor of mind, prompting Justice Frankfurter to note: "He speaks with force, he marshals his argument with power and his old habit of precision of detail is evident and when he has occasion to refer to a book or an argument, he produces it, he is sure and precise."

My friend still has his vigor. He says he was trained very early to make no statement of fact without documentation. He divided lawyers into two groups. There are those who, when they undertake an assignment, enable you to cross that item from your list. And then there are those who, when they make a similar commitment, require you to make a notation to follow up.

We wondered whether we could identify a pattern of conduct that stands out from our day-to-day business of meeting with clients, filing papers, meeting deadlines, missing deadlines, having some luck, and missing some opportunities.

I offered up a comment by the British journalist and author Malcolm Muggeridge. In his book *The Sun Never Sets* Muggeridge writes about the events in Britain in the years leading up to World War II, looking for a pattern that explains how and why things happened as they did:

> The present is always chaos, its prophets always charlatans, its values always false. When it has become the past, and may be looked back on, only then is it possible to detect order underlying the chaos, truth underlying the charlatanry, inexorable justice underlying the false values. That man had to speak and that man to be silent, that man had to rise to power and that man fall, that victory had to be won and that defeat suffered. Looked back on, the past makes a *pattern*, every element of which, however trivial, is necessary to the whole; each incident, each word spoken, the tilt of each hat, the modulation of each voice, falling into its place. Then it is apparent that nothing takes place aimlessly, no one exists aimlessly; that truly the hairs of each head have been numbered, and the fall of each sparrow to the ground, foreseen.

A pattern I now can identify commenced in the early 1960's when lawyers practiced law as general partners. At about that time Congress, by statute, gave corporations a tax benefit that was available only to corporations. The Bar of the various states adopted a model Professional Corporation in order to get the tax benefit. However, there was an interesting throw-in: corporate protection against personal liability. Those few words put an end to the civility of the general partnership where each partner was the agent of the other and each partner's own personal wealth was on the line. In a professional corporation the lawyers are employees and get corporate protection. This gradually moved the practice of law into the culture of the corporate marketplace. When the tax statutes were changed and there was no longer a need for the corporate paperwork, the law firms, state by state, created the hybrid we have now, the limited liability partnership. It gives the advantages of the partnership and the advantages of corporate protection.

We went from the IBM Selectrics, carbon paper, five onion-skin copies, and low overhead to the computer technology, 65 percent overhead, and 200-page LLP partnership agreements, providing for the expulsion of a partner "for no reason." The only action that remains to complete the pattern is a public offering. I read somewhere that law firms in Australia have done something like that, and the solicitors in Great Britain are looking into it.

There continues to be a thriving old-style law practice that is separate from the marketplace. It consists of lawyers who vindicate constitutional rights, lawyers in small firms who practice in the counties surrounding the big cities, the specialty lawyers in domestic relations, personnel matters, and probate matters. However, it is the marketplace firms that define the big-city practice.

What does one learn from years of practice? Is there advice that can be passed on to those on the way up, apart from the platitudes? The only advice I have come up with is that you make your own mistakes and correct a few and move on.

On my office door is advice that has worked for me. Perhaps it may work for you.

- Be kind, for everyone you meet is fighting a great battle.
- Most irrationality has some connection, however attenuated, with reality.
- Nothing is ever quite as good or as bad as the prevailing mood of the moment.
- Read the statute and read the rules.

- [I]n almost every case except the very plainest, it would be possible to decide the issue either way with reasonable legal justification.
  Lord Macmillan

- This day I shall have to do with an idle curious vain man, with an unthankful man, with a talkative railer, a crafty, false or an envious man. An unsociable sarcastic man. A greedy man. A deceiver. Such is the way of the world, and I shall be no more affected by it than I am about changes in the weather.
  Marcus Aurelius (Stein translation from the Latin)

And my favorite—
- A moment's insight is sometimes worth a life's experience.
  Oliver Wendell Holmes Jr.

BOOKS

The only books that influence us are those for which we
are ready, and which have gone a little farther down our
particular path than we have yet got ourselves.

E. M. Forster

That codeless myriad of precedent,
That wilderness of single instances,
Through which a few, by wit or fortune led,
May beat a pathway out to wealth and fame.

Alfred, Lord Tennyson

A BOOK ON THE BUS

As I leave my house in the morning to take the bus to the office, I take a book with me. The bus is a good place to read. There is isolation. There is no need to fight the traffic or watch out for pedestrians on cell phones. The bicyclists entertain with their twists and turns, all done with the skill of a Spanish toreador.

The book this morning is *Ten Theories of Human Nature* by Leslie Forster Stevenson and David L. Haberman. The sales slip tells me I purchased it four years ago. I never opened it. I am tempted to buy any book whose title includes the words "human nature." Whether I will read it is another question.

The title, Ten Theories of Human Nature, is followed by a list of ten sources of expertise on human nature: *Confucianism, Hinduism, The Bible, Plato, Aristotle, Kant, Marx, Freud, Sartre,* and *Darwinism.*

The authors could have added the Common Law theory of human nature. It is a belief in free will and the reasonably prudent man. Those who elect to depart from this standard face a variety of sanctions. In short, we must behave ourselves in accordance with the *res gestae.*

As I read, I am distracted by rain drops collecting on the bus windows. I had hoped to get to the office without taking an umbrella—I was wrong. Although the sky is dark, there are breaks in the clouds. Will the rain stop before I get off at Connecticut Avenue and K Street? That is the big question at this moment in my life, not the ten theories of human nature. The bus driver has yet to put on his windshield wipers, a comforting sign.

Now back to the book. It says any respectable theory of human nature must deal with these four areas:

- The nature of this world and our place in it
- What is so distinctive about us as compared to the other things in this world
- The ills of humanity
- The way to cure these ills

In considering the ills, the authors bring up, for example, the fact of human selfishness. I have thought about selfishness many times over the years. A substantial part of the litigation I see turns on the selfishness of the litigants, especially in cases involving wills and estates. Each related survivor wants what the other has. Is selfishness a constituent element in our makeup? Is it in our DNA, as scientist, researcher, and theorist Mr. E. O. Wilson suggests, and if it is, how do we cope with it?

It's still raining. I see people on the bus who were sensible enough to bring an umbrella. Some of the umbrellas are small enough to be carried in a briefcase. They offer little protection.

Other passengers have the big, widespread, gaudily colored golf umbrellas. They offer protection against a torrential rainstorm.

I see a passenger who has the English gentleman's style umbrella, black with a curled bamboo handle. An umbrella like that, the genuine article like the one carried by Sherlock Holmes, costs a couple of hundred dollars at today's prices.

I have left good umbrellas on the bus more times than I can remember. However, I have never called Metro's Lost and Found Office to inquire about my umbrella. That is not my human nature. I cope by telling myself the umbrella will find its way to someone who needs it.

We are now at 21st and K, and it is still raining. Finally, the bus driver has put on the wipers. Traffic has been stopped for 10 minutes. The driver is letting people rush off before reaching the next designated bus stop.

I am in no rush. I keep the vain hope that the rain will stop before we reach my stop at Connecticut and K. If the rain doesn't stop, I will run the one block to my office at Connecticut and L.

I turn again to the book on human nature. So far, I have read only 10 pages. I decide to skip to page 244 where the authors give their concluding thoughts:

> Besides naming and opposing evil, we can do something more positive by putting forward and upholding standards of goodness, expressing our ideals of how human life ought to be. Again, "preaching" may be objectionable, and the first duty is to try to embody or emulate those ideals ourselves: as the old saying has it, "actions speak louder than words." But, given our social nature and our individual fallibility, there is a need for

some attempt at institutional, permanent, or ongoing presentation of ideals and some kind of spiritual practice to help people rise to them.

While drying off in my office, I think it appropriate to any consideration of human nature to locate H. L. Mencken's January 22, 1925, letter to Sara P. Haardt (he later married her), directed to her in the sanitarium where she was under treatment for tuberculosis.

Perhaps I should send a copy of Mencken's letter to the authors of *Ten Theories of Human Nature*. Mencken is all for cynicism as "the most comforting of philosophies. You [Sara Haardt] will get over your present difficulties only to run into something worse, and so on, until the last sad scene. Make up your mind to it—and then make the best of it."

Mencken closes the letter saying that life remains livable despite its troubles. "Biological necessities keep us going. It is the feeling of exerting effort that exhilarates us, as a grasshopper is exhilarated by jumping. A hard job, full of impediments, is thus more satisfying than an easy job. ... But I run on á la Polonius.

"Please excuse poor pen."

A HAPPY MOMENT
IN THE LAW LIBRARY

I t has been said that happiness in life is based 10 percent on what happens and 90 percent on how you react to it. In other words happiness depends on the 90% within your control. You are the ultimate judge of what reality really is. You define what the world is all about. As the Stoics say, nothing happens until you, yourself, decide what happens. Would a busy lawyer with a demanding practice filled with uncertainty adopt the 90/10 ratio? Before doing the math, let us define happiness.

Lin Yutang in his book, *The Importance of Living*, writes about happiness from the point of view of the Chinese sages. Lin has looked at the pictures of the contented old man sitting in his boat gazing into the mists that conceal distant snow-covered mountains where wisdom and contentment reside. Lin concludes that happiness is associated with the proper functioning of the biological. It is a matter of digestion. It is removing a stone from the shoe.

He says: "In this world of ours, happiness is very often negative, the complete absence of sorrow or mortification or bodily ailment." No creditor at the door and nobody sick at home is happiness enough for the wise. Lin supports his statement by the expert testimony of Chin Shengt'an, a Chinese writer of the seventeenth century who enumerated thirty-three happy moments of his life. Here are two selections:

I wake up one morning and seem
to hear someone in the house sighing
and saying that last night someone died.
I immediately ask to find out who it is, and
learn that it is the sharpest, most calculating
fellow in town. Ah, is this not happiness?
I am drinking on a winter's night, and
suddenly note the night has turned
extremely cold. I push open the
window and see that snowflakes
come down the size of a palm and
there are already three or four inches
of snow on the ground. Ah, is this not happiness?

In Chinese paintings of happy moments, a snowstorm often plays a part. A snowstorm figured in one of my happy moments, a happy moment that only a procrastinating lawyer (is there any other kind?) can fully appreciate.

On a Sunday afternoon in gray November, I was in the Bar Association library preparing instructions in a case to be tried Monday. These instructions should have been worked up months ago. The legal issues in the case were tangled around knotty concepts of anticipatory breach of contract, mitigation of damages, and failure to perform. The authorities were contradictory. The leading cases were long in the opinion and short in the logic. The dissents set forth my position and cited cases in old reports where the views of the court were set forth in page after page of double columnar agate type.

A sense of panic seized me. I realized I would be in the library for hours just reading the cases. It would take hours more to summarize them so that I could defend the convoluted instructions that were necessary in order for me to prevail.

I glanced out the window. The skies were dark. Snow was falling. I arraign myself for not preparing this case when it could have been done leisurely and carefully. I should have read the cases over and then discussed them with my partner. I should have refined draft after draft of the key instructions. That is the proper way to prepare a case such as this. I will never let myself fall into this trap again. As the snow picked up I thought that maybe the snowstorm would become so heavy that the courts would close down. A vain hope. The snow was mixed with rain.

My thoughts were interrupted by the librarian. He whispered that I was wanted on the telephone. It must be a mistake, I thought. I walked over to the librarian's desk. I picked up the phone. It was for me. It was my opponent. His client had decided to accept our offer. The case was settled. I was free. I could leave Williston unread and Corbin on the desk unopened. I could walk amid the snowflakes kicking the slush, carefree and easy of conscience.

I entered that call in my good luck escrow account. Each time I make such an entry I am concerned that I am drawing against an account in danger of an overdraft. Is there any way of replenishing the good luck account? There may be. Do something good for somebody and do it anonymously. For instance you are retained in a case where your adversary, an overworked good person, let the statute of limitations run on his client's case. If you plead the statute he will be sued for malpractice. You convince your client not to plead it. You try the case strictly on the merits and win it. Ah, is this not happiness?

Lawyers aspire to remain serene despite the fact that we are immersed in other people's problems. Add to it our own problems. And add that our adversary is determined to make trouble for us. I would say 40/60 is about right for what happened to me last week.

A PERSONAL CREED

O n a bookshelf in my office rests the Yale University Press volumes of the papers of Benjamin Franklin. I came across the books when I was in Philadelphia in 1968 attending an American Bar Association convention. I ran into a cynical friend of mine in the convention hotel's lobby. He said if I wanted to form an organization where the members have no connection with the way the organization is run, I should study the controlling documents of the ABA.

This gave me the excuse I needed to leave the hotel and wander around Philadelphia. My wanderings took me to a bookstore devoted to Benjamin Franklin. Among the Franklin books were the Yale University Press publications. I signed up for the whole works, as issued.

Years later I put in a stop order at volume 27. Many more volumes have been published. Perhaps the set now runs into 50 volumes with more to come. Franklin's papers still turn up in attics and cellars all over the world.

Franklin continues to tantalize biographers. Every aspect of his long life has been studied by specialists, his women friends in Paris and London, his negotiations with the French and the English, his enemies, his role as a founding father, his troubled relationship with his son William.

We now have Edmund S. Morgan's readable mature summary of Franklin in the round. Morgan leaves to the other biographers the minute details.

Franklin would have made a good lawyer. He was intelligent and energetic, and he saw life as a series of tests, cases perhaps, to be studied and solved.

He was an intensely practical man. He did not waste time with what might have been or with the wish to be on the other side of the case where the facts were better. He was where he was and he must work with what he had. He conducted himself in the spirit of a statement attributed to General George C. Marshall: "Repeating that we are surrounded does not qualify as a plan of escape."

When his stove smoked up his house, he set to work to invent a better stove. When he made his discoveries about electricity, he put what he learned to work by designing the lightning rod. He experimented on himself by trying vegetarianism and other dietary regimes; he tried cold air baths in the morning to prevent head colds.

He wanted to know the best way to get on in this troubled, competitive, contentious world. We have his answer to the question in the form of his personal creed, published in his autobiography.

How many of us would take the time to write out the principles that guide us in our everyday activities?

Here is Franklin's attempt:

1. Temperance.

Eat not to Dulness. Drink not to Elevation.

2. Silence.

Speak not but what may benefit others or yourself.
Avoid trifling Conversation.

3. Order.

Let all your Things have their Places.
Let each Part of your Business have its Time.

4. Resolution.

Resolve to perform what you ought.
Perform without fail what you resolve.

5. Frugality.

Make no Expense but to do good to others or yourself i.e.
Waste nothing.

6. Industry.

Lose no Time. Be always employ'd in something useful.
Cut off all unnecessary Actions.

7. Sincerity.

Use no hurtful Deceit.
Think innocently and justly; and, if you speak, speak accordingly.

8. Justice.

Wrong none, by doing Injuries or omitting the
Benefits that are your Duty.

9. Moderation.

Avoid Extreams. Forbear resenting Injuries so much as
you think they deserve.

10. Cleanliness.

Tolerate no Uncleanness in Body, Cloaths or Habitation.

11. Tranquility.

Be not disturbed at Trifles, or at Accidents common or unavoidable.

12. Chastity.

Rarely use Venery but for Health or Offspring; Never to Dulness, Weakness, or the Injury of your own or another's Peace or Reputation.

13. Humility.

Imitate Jesus and Socrates.

What would Franklin say about John Adams' accusation that Franklin at heart was nothing but a manipulator? What was the real story of his estrangement from his son William? Why did he buy so much wine? Why is there no evidence of a marriage certificate recording his marriage to Deborah Read? Would we get answers or would we be met with infinite resources of silence? See his number 2 above.

What would Franklin say ...

BOOKS

Occasionally an odd volume of the *Federal Reporter* finds its way to a used bookstore. Its presence there means that somewhere a law library is disfigured by the gap left by this prodigal that detached itself from its companions and wandered far away.

I was once tempted to buy such strays and start up a collection of the *Federal Reporter* made up entirely of odd volumes. I tried it awhile, but I saw it was futile to believe I would live long enough to put together such a set. Nevertheless, I continue to examine the odd volumes I run across to see if there is a way of telling, by a business card used as a bookmark, who was the lawyer who once owned the book. Twice I have had the pleasure of returning a book to its owner.

What I shall relate to you now concerns volume 242 F.2d. I saw it in a local used bookstore. I took it from the shelf. I leafed through it to see if there was identification of the previous owner. I saw none. What I did see was a decision directly on point concerning a products liability case that was bothering me. The case dealt with the duty to third parties of a remote manufacturer of a defective product. The opinion, with clarity, brevity, and precision, held that the manufacturer was absolutely liable.

I made a note of the page number in 242 F.2d, so I could bring it up on Lexis. When I punched in the citation nothing appeared. I tried other search methods. Still nothing. I went to the bar library to examine its volume. The case I was looking for was not where it should have been.

I returned to the bookstore. I bought volume 242 F.2d. I took the book to the bar library to make a comparison. It was then that I noticed the book I had just purchased had a strangeness about it. The reds and blacks on the spine were of stunning brilliance.

The book was filled with cases deciding issues that needed deciding but were as yet untouched by legitimate judicial illumination. Each opinion was beautifully written and filled with sweet reasonableness. There was a long opinion reversing the trial court and in the process solving the vexing problem of ownership of joint bank accounts. Near the end of the book was a case that once and for all clarified the law concerning due process and out-of-state defendants. Each point was amply footnoted. The counterfeiter had the presumption to place dissents after several of the majority opinions. The strident language of one of the dissents would qualify as a dissent by a certain Supreme Court Justice.

I noticed that the counterfeiter placed on the lower section of the book's spine the words "In Memoriam to Judge Joseph Force Crater." In the front of the book were eulogies delivered by two of Judge Crater's law clerks. One stated that the judge had been an active and successful trial lawyer with the well-known international firm of Vellschmerz & Schadenfreude before he was appointed to the federal court. Judge Crater was eulogized as a distinguished trial judge who expired in his chambers after putting in a full day dealing with the long motions calendar. As was his practice, he took nothing under advisement. Each motion was decided from the bench. He was a model of courtesy. He was beloved by the bar.

The name Judge Crater had a familiar ring. Judge Crater. Yes, that was the name of the New York State Supreme Court judge who was last seen on August 6, 1930, hailing a cab in front of the New York Public Library. Judge Crater's disappearance was the subject of media speculation for years afterward. It was the 1930's version of the Jimmy Hoffa disappearance. The author of the counterfeit volume supplied at least one answer to the Judge Crater mystery. He had been killed off by long motions.

Was this book in my hand the only volume the counterfeiter had written, or was the hoax a continuing one? Was the energy of the counterfeiter so great that he had written an entire set of the *Federal Reporter*? The book contained no identifying marks. I thought that a specialist in bookbinding could give me some idea of the firm that did the binding job and that would lead me to the culprit. No luck. It was a blind alley.

I then speculated on what motive lay behind this clever performance. I noticed that the opinions and dissents demonstrated how a slight change in the use of a word or the alteration of a fact determined whether the court of appeals affirmed or reversed the trial judge. Could it be that the author was a trial judge retaliating against a court of appeals that had reversed him once too often?

I must turn to orthodox research. The authentic writing in volume 242 F.2d is lifeless compared to the fraudulent, for it is writing that—

... flooded the crimson twilight,
Like the close of an angel's psalm,
And it lay on my fevered spirit
With a touch of infinite calm. ...
It linked all perplexed meanings
Into one perfect peace,
And trembled away into silence
As if it were loath to cease.
I have sought, but I seek it vainly,
That one lost chord divine. ...

Adelaide Procter, *A Lost Chord*

LAWYERS IN QUOTES

Some 45 years ago I commenced collecting quotation anthologies. It became an obsession.

As the books came my way I usually flipped to the index to see whether there was something new concerning lawyers. It is rare to turn up something new. Each collection repeats what is in the others. The quotation never omitted is Shakespeare's "The first thing we do is kill all the lawyers." All educated people know Shakespeare did not intend to disparage lawyers by the remark. He wished to demonstrate that the quickest way to anarchy was to kill all the lawyers. Without lawyers there is mob rule.

The other quotation most frequently found is St. Paul's: "It is altogether a defect in you that you have lawsuits one with the other."

A number of quotations follow on St. Paul's condemnation of litigation. Judge Learned Hand's is the most striking: "I must say that, as a litigant, I should dread a lawsuit beyond almost

York Times. It said that Victor de Guinzbourg, a member of the United Nations staff, had published a collection of proverbs and quotations of all nations. I bought a copy. It turned out to be an oversized book with a yellow cover. I see it now sitting on a shelf right across the room. In it I found something of interest to the criminal lawyer who must deal with clumsy attempts at client cover-up stories. I quote from de Guinzbourg's book:

> In the old days, a king known for his cruelty demanded that his court jester illustrate, within the hour, the meaning of the proverb "The explanation is often worse than the crime itself," or the king would torture the jester to death.
>
> As the king and his queen, attired in royal robes, were some time later slowly mounting a staircase, the jester stole behind them and gave the king a loving pinch. The king, with sword drawn, wheeled around and was about to decapitate the fool, who yelled:
>
> "Sorry, Your Majesty, I thought it was the Queen!"

Experienced criminal lawyers are apprehensive when their clients give explanations because he who explains confesses. It is a thought well understood from the earliest times:

> "Never make a defense or apology before you be accused."
>
> Charles I, Letter to Lord Wentworth, September 3, 1636

THE LAW IN STYLE

A unique byproduct of the common-law tradition is the large body of legal writing known as reported case law. I am told that jurisdictions that follow a different tradition, the reliance on a predetermined legislative code to decide all cases, do not need shelf on shelf of law books because precedent is not a significant consideration. A good sampling of what the common law has given us is between the covers of the recently published *Oxford Dictionary of American Legal Quotations*, by Fred R. Shapiro. Here we find the austere simplicity of Oliver Wendell Homes Jr., contrasted with the embroidered rococo of writers such as Judge Michael A. Musmanno.

Judge Musmanno is on display in condemning Henry Miller's *Tropic of Cancer*:

> "Cancer" is not a book. It is a cesspool, an open sewer, a pit of putrefaction, a slimy gathering of all that is rotten in the debris of human depravity. And in the center of all this waste and stench, besmearing himself with

its foulest defilement, splashes, leaps, cavorts and wallows a bifurcated specimen that responds to the name of Henry Miller. One wonders how the human species could have produced so lecherous, blasphemous, disgusting and amoral a human being as Henry Miller. One wonders why he is received in polite society.

Michael A. Musmanno, *Commonwealth v. Robin*,
421 Pa. 70, 91, 218 A.2d 546 (1966) (dissenting)

I met Judge Musmanno thirty years ago. He was then a man in his sixties, rather thin, energetic, and distinguished-looking. He sported a black cape. Flowing gray hair peeked out from a black slouch hat.

The Musmanno style brought to mind Judge Henry Lamm, and I turned to the index and there he was, to be found on page 419 speaking of "witnesses" and "truth":

Truth does not always stalk boldly forth naked, but with modest withal, in a printed abstract in a court of last resort. She oft hides in nooks and crannies visible only to the mind's eye of the judge who tries the case. To him appears the furtive glance, the blush of conscious shame, the hesitation, the sincere or the flippant or sneering tone, the heat, the calmness, the yawn, the sigh, the candor or lack of it, the scant or full realization of the solemnity of an oath, the carriage and mien. The brazen face of the liar, the glibness of the schooled witness in reciting a lesson or the itching over-eagerness of the swift witness, as well as honest face of the truthful one, are alone seen by him. In short, one witness may give testimony that reads in print, here, as falling from

24

the lips of an angel of light and may testify so that it reads brokenly and obscurely in print, and yet there was that about the witness that carried conviction of truth to every soul who heard him testify.

Henry Lamm, *Creamer v. Bivert*,

214 Mo. 473,479–80, 113S.W. 1118(1908)

Although most quotations are taken from reported cases, a goodly number represent writers who are not lawyers. Mark Twain appears fifty-three times, the same number of times as Justice William J. Brennan Jr.; Will Rogers twenty-one times. While perusing I saw references to Judge Logan E. Bleckley, a new name to me. He, too, appears twenty-one times and is particularly eloquent concerning juries:...

> Left to exercise their common-sense in their own way, the jury will generally determine correctly what is well-proved, and what lacks further support. Furnished with a superfluity of rules, their attention is distracted and the proffered help only obstructs. The better practice is, to decline charging refined speculations, and give only coarse, sharp-cut law. What shall come to the jury as evidence, is for the court. What it is worth when it arrives, is for the jury.

Logan E. Bleckley, *Moughon v. State*,

7Ga. 102,106(1876)

Bleckley's reassuring comment about juries is balanced by a comment not included in the *Oxford Dictionary*. An experienced criminal lawyer told me I should never despair when defending a man charged with indecency: "Six of the jury won't believe that such things happen, and the other six will go home and try it themselves."

I searched the index in vain for quotations from the writings of Judge Bruce Selya of the First Circuit. His spectacular vocabulary is the subject of a note in the *Scribes Journal of Legal Writing*, Volume 2. The writer chides Judge Selya for his use of such words as "decurtate," "encincture," "eschatocol," and others known only to Judge Selya and William Buckley. This brings me back to Oliver Wendell Holmes Jr., at page 185:

> The former secretaries, who adore the Justice, delight in such stories. One of them objected to the phrasing of a certain opinion, maintaining that the shading given to one word meant that "there isn't more than one man in a thousand who will understand it." "I write for that man," the Justice retorted.
>
> *Justice Oliver Wendell Holmes* by Silas Bent

Perhaps Judge Selya writes for that one man. Justice Holmes is the most often quoted in the *Dictionary of American Legal Quotations*. Justice Robert H. Jackson is second. There are similarities in the writing styles. Both take the practical view of things. Both distrust absolutes and both have no use for those who claim a monopoly on truth. Justice Jackson also has good things to say about lawyers. One of the kindest is the Harrison Tweed quote about lawyers, also found in the *Oxford Dictionary*:

I have a high opinion of lawyers. With all their faults, they stack up well against those in every other occupation or profession. They are better to work with or play with or fight with or drink with than most other varieties of mankind.

LEGAL REASONING—
THE SWEET SCIENCE

"Induction," one of them insisted.
"Deduction," cried another.
"Analogy," suggested the mildest of the party.
"Strict construction," answered yet another.
I, too, became intoxicated by these legal reasoning words.
"Rationalization!" I chimed in, "Original intention!"
"Deviation!" "Interpretation!"

Variations on a Theme by Logan Pearsall Smith

In 1955 I had a Congressional Library stack pass. With it I could wander as I pleased along the fabulous stacks of one of the great libraries of the world. In my strolls through the law division I noticed odd-looking law books that had the word science in the title. *The Science and Logic of Pleading, The Science of Proof, The Science of Legal Rhetoric.* These books were either privately printed or published by local publishers. They bore publication dates from the 1800's to the 1940's. The common thread was the author's wish to elevate legal reasoning to a mathematical science. Common-law pleading, so it was said, was pure logic, Euclidean logic inevitably leading to ergo.

We do not see such books anymore. If math were a required law school subject, many of us would not be practicing law and the law schools would have fewer applicants.

At the January Senate Judiciary Committee hearing concerning a Supreme Court nominee, the nominee had to endure hours of pointed questions concerning his early beliefs and writings. Nevertheless the senators were kind enough to refrain from asking him the most difficult question of all: "Judge, would you take a few minutes and tell us just what legal reasoning is."

If such a question were asked, there would have been a respectable period of silence as the witness collected his thoughts. Just what legal reasoning is defies a clear, unambiguous definition.

As I write I have before me my collection of books dealing with the subject. You will understand from the titles why the judge would have paused: *The Nature of the Judicial Process* by Benjamin N. Cardozo (1921); *The Folklore of Capitalism* by Thurman Arnold (1937); *Law and Other Things* by Lord Macmillan (1939); *The Mysterious Science of the Law* by Daniel J. Boorstin (1941); *Think Clearly* by Moxley and Fife (1941); *An Introduction to Legal Reasoning* by Edward H. Levi (1948); *The Nature of Legal Argument* by O. C. Jensen (1957); *Law as Large as Life: A Natural Law for Today and the Supreme Court as Its Prophet* by Charles P. Curtis (1959); *The Rules of Chaos* by Stephen Vizinczey (1969); *Law and Morality* edited by Louis Blom-Cooper and Gavin Drewry (1976); *Tactics of Legal Reasoning* by Pierre Schlag and David Skover (1986); *Logic for Lawyers: A Guide to Clear Legal Thinking* by Ruggero J. Aldisert (1989); *The Problems of Jurisprudence* by

Richard A. Posner (1990); *Unreason Within Reason: Essays on the Outskirts of Rationality* by A. C. Graham (1992); *An Introduction to Law and Legal Reasoning* by Steven J. Burton (1995); *Imagining the Law: Common Law and the Foundations of the American Legal System* by Norman F. Cantor (1997); and *A Clearing in the Forest: Law, Life and Mind* by Steven L. Winter (2001).

Thurman Arnold, in *The Folklore of Capitalism*, says legal reasoning is a branch of literature and folklore. He cites Justice Cardozo.

Judge Aldisert is defiant in asserting that legal reasoning follows a system of logic using induction, deduction, and analogy. In his book he points out the logical flaws in the opinions of his fellow judges, who really do not understand legal reasoning.

Levi's book, *An Introduction to Legal Reasoning*, is often referred to as a good statement of what the law is. He opens the discussion with restraint:

> This is an attempt to describe generally the process of legal reasoning in the field of case law and in the interpretation of statutes and of the Constitution. It is important that the mechanism of legal reasoning should not be concealed by its pretense. The pretense is that the law is a system of known rules applied by a judge; the pretense has long been under attack. In an important sense legal rules are never clear, and, if a rule had to be clear before it could be imposed, society would be impossible.

In *Law and Morality*, edited by Blom-Cooper and Drewry, we read of the bitter fight between Oliver Wendell Holmes Jr.'s group asserting that law must be separated from morality and

Lord Devlin's group asserting that law rests on a stable and iden-
tifiable community sentiment of what is moral and what is right.
Lord Devlin says that the morals of society are the standards of
conduct of which the reasonable man approves. Common morality depends upon the collective wisdom or unwisdom of reasonable men.

Jensen, in *The Nature of Legal Argument*, says it is a mistake
to assume, as many do, that judicial decisions are logically derived
with mathematical, logical, and scientific precision. Jensen says
that human nature often contradicts such precision. Therefore
sensible legal reasoning partakes of common sense and a sense of
equity lest the ends of justice are defeated.

Let us say to those who would like law to be a science that
it is one of the sweet sciences, located somewhere between astrol-
ogy and astrophysics and not too far from its sibling, political
science.

WHAT TO DO
WHILE WAITING

To get his name on the title page of a useful law book has always been recognized as one of the few legitimate methods of publicity open to an aspiring member of the Bar.

Lord Macmillan

When I commenced practicing law, I had a lot of time on my hands. I decided to write a book. I was going to write about tort law in the District of Columbia.

When a case did come my way, for instance, one involving a slip and fall in a grocery store, there was no law book that identified such a case by the facts rather than the subject of "negligence" and "contributory negligence." To compile such a book I read every decided District of Columbia tort case and reclassified each under a common sense category.

It took me two years to read all the appellate cases, make notes on three-by-five cards, and transfer this information into book form.

What did I learn from reading all those cases? Well, I learned that, to get a verdict, a customer in a grocery store who slips and falls on a stray green bean and suffers a broken leg must prove that the grocery store had noticed the vegetable on the floor in sufficient time to clean it up.

I learned that in an automobile collision, the plaintiff must have looked in all directions at the same time (an impossibility) or he was contributorily negligent.

My book was titled *District of Columbia Tort Casefinder.* The "Preface," written long ago, takes into account the significance of a legal precedent in the common law. Here it is:

About the time of the American Revolution, Samuel Johnson, the English lexicographer, was having a conversation with a lawyer friend. Notes on the conversation were taken down by Johnson's shadow, Boswell, and later transcribed into Boswell's journals. Johnson passed the comment that when there were few precedents, there was an emphasis on the ability to reason logically, but with the increase of precedents (keep in mind this is about 1776), the skill of a lawyer depended less on his ability to reason and more on his ability to cite a controlling precedent. If that was true when Johnson said it, what is the situation today?

There are two factors which tend to eliminate the part played by legal reasoning and forensics in the present-day trial. First, there is the backlog of cases. Judges just do not have time to hear learned counsel spin out their views as to why a proposition should prevail. Second, there are now so many decided cases that there is a precedent available for almost any situation.

Finding the precedent is, of course, the difficulty.

Most of the colloquy between court and counsel terminates with the judge saying, "Do you have a local case on that point?" If you do, fine; if you don't, you may reason like Cicero, but you will not prevail over your opponent who, in a whisper, gives the court the controlling authority.

It is the purpose of this book to give you immediate access to the rulings in the field of torts by the Court of Appeals for the District of Columbia, as concisely and accurately as possible. This book should be particularly valuable when a crisis in the courtroom is announced by the judge, "Do you have a case on that point?"

To get the greatest benefit from this book, you should become familiar with its list of topics. The main categories are found under common sense headings, i.e., the factual situations. For instance, if you have a "fall" case, you look under FALLS. If you have a case where someone is struck by a hockey puck, you look under HOCKEY.

There was not a large market for the book. However, plaintiff lawyers and insurance defense lawyers bought copies to carry in their briefcases. What was most pleasing to me, however, was that trial judges also kept the book handy.

I often received emergency calls from friends who were at the courthouse during a recess requesting a citation right away.

I donated a copy to the Bar Association library located in the courthouse. The librarian would call me from time to time to tell me his copy had been stolen and would I bring down another.

The book remained in print with yearly supplements until LexisNexis and Westlaw made it obsolete. Nevertheless, I still get an occasional call asking for "that book, you know, that casefinder book."

Sorry, it is out of print.

ZEN AND THE ART OF PRACTICING LAW

Why not? There is *Zen and The Art of Archery* and many other Zens and The Art Of. What is there about Zen that gives it the right to attach itself to any subject it chooses and invest it with mystery? From what I have read Zen is a strategy for dealing with life's chaos. Zen does not exist in its pure state. It is like the ubiquitous element sodium. It is everywhere but nowhere because it combines with whatever it is close to. Most of us live and die without ever seeing, tasting, or touching pure sodium. We see lots of salt that contains sodium. But sodium, the native element, no. The pure stuff immediately combines with oxygen when it hits the air. The same may be true of Zen. It combines with whatever there is.

What happens when Zen combines with the law practice? It may provide objectivity. It may indicate what is worthwhile in each working day as we contend with the chaos devised by our cunning adversaries.

It may explain why we feel bad or good about a case. In some cases we happen to be on the side of right. In other cases the wrong side. In most cases nobody can tell who is clearly right or wrong. Even when we are on the right side, it may be a case with no moral significance, and should truth prevail it is a truth insignificant to all but the contestants.

Then there is the Zen of the case we lose, but the loss is better than the winning would have been.

I see my Zen this way. When we are on the right side, both morally and on the facts, and when our presence provides help that otherwise would not be there, it is then that the lawyer has a calling. It is a calling because nobody else will answer the call to correct an injustice. There may be little or no compensation. There may be criticism by those in brief authority. None of us has the capacity or the economic independence to undertake many such cases. Long hours may be required with little chance of success.

The purity of the endeavor is the Zen. The application of competence to a worthwhile cause transforms chaos into order.

In 1974 *Zen and the Art of Motorcycle Maintenance* appeared, written by Robert M. Pirsig, the son of a law school professor with a special interest in legal ethics. Pirsig's book is a philosophical novel, a speculation on the nature of quality, which Pirsig identifies as the Zen factor. Motorcycle maintenance is the metaphor for dealing with one's own life and the way it falls apart and requires quality maintenance. As Pirsig says, "The real cycle you're working on is a cycle called yourself."

Although the book starts slowly, and requires staying power, it is worth reading. It has sold well over three million copies. Pirsig falters in his effort to articulate a clear philosophy of quality, but what he does accomplish is instructive.

In discussing the things that destroy competence, Pirsig picks up the subject of why we don't do competent work. He introduces the concept of gumption, which he says is roughly equivalent to enthusiasm. Gumption leaks out because of gumption traps. "What I have in mind now is a catalog of 'Gumption Traps I Have Known.' I want to start a whole new academic field, gumptionology, in which these traps are sorted, classified, structured into hierarchies and interrelated for the edification of future generations and the benefit of all mankind."

We are all in the process of building up and running out of gumption. In applying Pirsig's concepts to law practice, I use as an illustration a case in which I commence with great enthusiasm. I file a complaint in full compliance with the federal rules. Gumption running high. Then I discover I cannot find the defendants to serve them. Where are they? A gumption trap. I need a special process server. More gumption used up.

Pirsig identifies the internal and external gumption traps. In the law practice the internal trap is related to self-doubt, boredom, and trying to do too much too quickly. The external trap is related to that wily adversary (our self) who thwarts the best-laid plans. After the success of *Zen and the Art of Motorcycle Maintenance* Pirsig published nothing for seventeen years. Then last year his second book, *Lila*, appeared. In it Pirsig continues to pursue the subject of competence and quality. *Lila* is not as thick with philosophical speculation as the earlier book. The title, *Lila*, is the name of a promiscuous woman who controls the lead character (Pirsig in disguise). Pirsig's treatment of the subject does not compare with W. Somerset Maugham's *Of Human Bondage*, or Marcel Proust's *Swann's Way*. But Pirsig's detour into his other obsession, competence and quality, in all its manifestations, saves the book.

CLIENTS

It is common knowledge that one of the first things an attorney does when a client seeks to secure his professional services is to establish the relation of attorney and client. All understand how this is accomplished.

In re Smith, 108 Fed. Rep. 39, *per* Purnell, J.

It is not the saints of the world who chiefly give employment to the legal profession.

In re Goodell, 39 Wis. 232, 20 Am. Rep. 42, *per* Ryan, C. J.

CLIENTS AND THE TRAIN TO NEW YORK

The Acela train ride from here to New York City is a pleasant trip. If it happens to be snowing outside it is all the better. I wish to speak about my last pleasant trip. Snow was falling and, in addition, I happened to sit next to an acquaintance who practiced law in New York City. We spoke in generalities on the way to Baltimore. Then we got down to serious business. We settled on the subject of clients. We composed a list of the clients a lawyer must avoid.

Here is our list, written on Acela notepaper:

—The one who says he has a perfect case. Send that one to a lawyer who specializes in perfect cases.

—The one a judge and jury will dislike. Send that one to a lawyer you dislike.

—The one who wants to know whether we are nasty enough for the case and whether we know how to fight in court. He wants to destroy his former partners. Send that one to a lawyer you really dislike.

—The one who says he would like to bring a lawsuit to get justice and is not interested in getting money. You might tell him that only the lucky few get justice, and he does not look like someone who is that lucky.

—The general counsel of the corporate client who says he hates the CEO and he, himself, would like to leave and join a law firm. There's a hot potato.

—The one who wants to sue a neighbor for defamation. Tell her that her neighbor probably has no money to pay a judgment.

—The one who has received a subpoena for documents, and asks "What would happen if these documents happen to get lost?" Send that one to a former prosecutor you dislike.

—The one who has a briefcase filled with letters with the envelopes attached. The attachment of the envelope to the letter is a clear symptom that the prospective client is suffering from a severe case of paranoia. The way to end the interview is to start peeling the envelopes from the letter. The prospective client will grab back the envelopes, and will immediately leave the office. Send that one to a paranoid lawyer.

—The one who wishes to move for a new trial, or take an appeal, in a case that has been lost, and prior counsel got all the money in fees. Tell him you could have really helped him out in the beginning, you could have won the case for him, but now it is too late.

—The one who has agreed to a settlement but has changed his mind and wants to switch lawyers. Tell him you know the lawyer and he knows what he is doing.

—The one who is dissatisfied with her third lawyer because he recommended that she settle her case. Tell her you don't take cases where you are the fourth lawyer.

—The one who says don't worry about your fee. That comment suggests that you will be well paid. Experience teaches that you will not be paid at all.

—The one who knows the CIA is tapping his phone and believes he's being followed. Refer him to a lawyer you dislike.

—The one who says he has already interviewed four other firms and he will make a decision in the next five days. Even if he were to select you he will be nothing but trouble.

I knew my acquaintance had a reputation in New York City as one of the lawyers to see when a lawyer has a problem of his own. Therefore I brought up the subject of lawyers as clients.

He said lawyers need lawyers because of a number of things. There may be an action brought by bar counsel alleging an ethical violation. There may be a case where a lawyer is sued for malpractice. There may be a case where a prosecutor is claiming that the attorney–client privilege does not apply because of the crime or fraud exception. There may be a case where a lawyer is in a dispute with his partners over the distribution of profits. There may be a case where a lawyer is going from one firm to another and taking clients with her.

We agreed that lawyers, most of the time, are easy clients to work with. This is because they are aware of the difficulties involved in any legal proceeding.

He said there was a case where he was representing a lawyer who had been sued for malpractice. There was to be a summary judgment hearing on the case. He called his client and asked him if he wanted to be present. The client said he did not want to be present. Just call him when the judge had ruled. The client added that if he were told that the judge took the bench and then tap danced on the bench and sang "Makin' Whoopee," he would not be surprised. Anything can happen in a legal proceeding. That is an understanding client.

He said that in New York City the overhead in the big firms is crushing. The lawyer who brings in the business does not want to contribute to that overhead, so he takes his group and his good clients over to a smaller firm where the overhead is one-half of what it is at the big firm. This produces partnership disputes. Such cases go to arbitration because all the LLP agreements have arbitration clauses.

I asked him how he developed the specialty of representing lawyers. He said he worked in a firm that represented one of the legal malpractice insurers. After a few years of that he started his own practice. He added that if he were going back to law school, he would make sure he took Partnership Law and Accounting.

By the time we approached Penn Station, the snow had stopped. "Make sure you have your belongings from the overhead racks. We will be in New York City in three minutes." A pleasant ride.

A FORENSIC FABLE

… perfectly at ease with himself and everyone around him, he managed at the same time to suggest the proximity of an abyss of scandal and bankruptcy threatening at any moment to engulf himself and anyone else unfortunate to be within his immediate vicinity when the crash came. The charm he exercised over people was perhaps largely due to this ability to juggle with two contrasting, apparently contradictory, attributes; the one, an underlying implication of sinister disturbing undercurrents; the other, a soothing power to reassure and entertain.

Anthony Powell

I have encountered in the trial practice the type of person that Anthony Powell, the novelist, describes. On occasion I have represented such a person. When I have, I was treated to flattery, lots of flattery, but slow pay. He would tell me, if it was a criminal case, he must suspend a lucrative transaction until I persuaded the prosecutor that the case against him was based on a vast misunderstanding of the documents and the incorrigible greed of the complaining witnesses.

He would mention the names of prominent lawyers he knew. He would ask—if and when the present matter was over—whether I would be willing to represent some very wealthy friend of his in a complicated international arbitration. Would I object to traveling to Paris, Rome, London, and Geneva?

I have a lawyer friend who represented many real estate speculators and investors. This brought him in touch with the Anthony Powell type. My friend complained that his clients did little work, made big money, and were not very smart. The clients used him more or less as a well-paid messenger boy. My friend's greed got the best of him. He left the law practice and joined up with a client in various financial schemes.

He sent me an announcement of the formation of the venture. His picture adorned the announcement. When next we met I noticed he had dropped the cautious vocabulary of a lawyer. Now his sentences began with the words "Roughly speaking."

Occasionally I received a call from my friend asking about one of the local rules of court. He said he represented a big venture in its litigation. He liked getting into court now and then and seeing the courthouse crowd.

Months later when I spoke to my friend, the sentences no longer commenced with the words "Roughly speaking." He wanted me to refer him to a lawyer concerning some out-of-state litigation. The venture had been sued. He said he was named a defendant. His partner and he could not use the same lawyer because of conflicts that had arisen between them. There were allegations of fraud.

This special type person I write about often gets drawn into litigation that commences with a complaint alleging fraud stated with the particularity required in accordance with Rule 9(b) of the Federal Rules of Civil Procedure. If the special type can muddy the waters, he may get away with all or part of his scheme. But there are cases where the special type does not do so well.

One such case is *Sankin v. 5410 Connecticut Ave. Corp.*, 282 F. Supp. 525 (1968). Here is the trial judge's reaction to the special type's winning ways on the witness stand:

> The hallmark of his testimony was evasion flavored with contradiction. Time after time he had to be directed to answer the question and not evade. And when be would be compelled to give an answer, it was usually an exercise in circumlocution. His appearance, manner, demeanor and conduct as a witness was that of a person unworthy of belief. He did not look nor did he act as a witness who was telling the truth fully, frankly and freely what he knew to be so.

Back to my lawyer friend. A year later I received an announcement that he resumed the practice of law.

The lesson: The shoemaker must stick to his last.

A NEW CASE ARRIVES

Does the name Lloyd Paul Stryker mean anything to you? Probably not. Let me tell you something about him. He conducted a successful one-man trial practice in New York City from the 1920's to the 1950's. He tried many criminal and civil headline cases.

Stryker had a colorful style. He did not believe in understatement. What he had to say he said loud and clear. In one of his appellate arguments the issue was wiretap evidence, a process that Justice Oliver Wendell Holmes Jr. in a dissenting opinion had characterized as "dirty business." Here is a contemporary description of Stryker's performance:

"Dirty, dirty business." he said, and, finding the phrase sweet to his lips he kept repeating it with mounting enthusiasm until the courthouse shook and one of the judges, managing somehow to make himself heard, called down, "Don't make so much noise; I can hear you."

49

Stryker responded by saying he was sorry that the tone of his voice annoyed the judge. He said he was unable to encounter an outrage such as wiretapping with complacence. "And yet I have one consolation. As I think back to that little Boston State House in February, 1761, when James Otis before a hostile court thundered against the Writs of Assistance, I am satisfied that he too on that occasion raised his voice."

I met Lloyd Paul Stryker. Not in person but through his book *The Art of Advocacy* published in 1954, a year before he died.

The book opens with a description of how it is to get a new case. He recalls a Broadway play about a lawyer who suffers one misfortune after another. In despair he climbs onto the window ledge preparatory to a fatal leap. As he is about to jump, the telephone rings. "The ringing interrupts his suicidal purpose. He decides to answer it. And as he answers it, he undergoes a sudden change; his back stiffens, his eyes flash, his voice loses its dull tone. The son of a great industrialist has just been arrested, charged with murder! Disconsolate and without hope a moment back, the lawyer suddenly has become like a spirited fire horse eager to throw his whole weight into the collar. His troubles are forgotten, a new case has arrived!"

A new case. What is it about? It usually involves money. Who has it? Who wants it?

As you listen to your new client you may speculate that There Go I but for the Grace of God. A thought that puts a brake against being judgmental.

In 1949, Lloyd Stryker got the famous Alger Hiss case. It did not involve money. It involved Alger Hiss's freedom. The press named it the case of the century. Hiss was a man of great accomplishment. A distinguished lawyer, he had served a clerkship with Oliver Wendell Holmes Jr. He had been employed with the Department of Justice, the Solicitor General's Office, and the State Department. He had accompanied President Franklin Roosevelt to the Yalta Conference where he met Churchill and Stalin. And now he was accused of being a communist and a Russian spy involved in espionage.

In 1948 Hiss appeared before a grand jury in New York and denied the charges. He was indicted on two counts of perjury. The chief government witness was Whittaker Chambers, a former communist and Russian spy. Chambers himself was a confessed perjurer.

Stryker and Hiss were different from each other. Stryker held nothing in reserve. He said what was on his mind both to courts and juries. Hiss was all reserve. Despite these differences, Stryker and Hiss formed a temporary alliance.

The trial commenced in 1949. The prosecutor, Thomas Murphy, made a tactical blunder. He declared in opening statement that the case turned on who the jury will believe—Hiss or Chambers. Stryker's strategy was to attack Chambers and exalt Hiss. The case ended in a hung jury.

The rumor was that after the trial Stryker told Hiss he thought he could get him another hung jury, but he did not think he could acquit him.

Hiss changed lawyers. In the re-trial the prosecution focused on the circumstantial evidence pointing to Hiss's guilt. The re-trial ended in a conviction.

In his book Stryker says that a new case may often punctuate a long drought. It is comforting to note that even the busiest lawyers have their dry periods when the phone does not ring.

Stryker used his downtime to write two biographies, one of President Andrew Johnson and the other of Thomas Erskine, an 18th century British barrister.

I would like to conclude my remarks with Mr. Stryker's concluding remarks to the jury in the Hiss case:

Ladies and gentlemen, I have been called florid-faced. They tell me I have grey hair. Alas, I am afraid it is true. It seems only a moment ago when people were commenting on my extreme youth. But with all my faults if I have offended any one of you in any way, hold it against me, not against Alger Hiss.

Ladies and gentlemen, the case will be in your hands. I beg you, I pray you to search your consciences and have no fear, "Yea, though I have walked to the valley of the shadow of death," in this case. Alger Hiss, this long nightmare is drawing to a close. Rest well. Your case, your life, your liberty are in good hands. Thank you.

The jury split 8 to 4 for conviction.

A SPECIAL CALENDAR

Hating people at a distance, hating people you have never met, is not for real haters. To really hate someone you must have known the hatee very well. Former law partners, former business partners, and estranged family members know how to hate each other. And when hate turns to "let's litigate," the litigation is hateful and nasty.

This nasty litigation carries two distinguishing features. First the complaint. Invariably the complaint alleges repeated instances of breach of trust, fraud, and sly threats of blackmail held in reserve. The second distinguishing feature is the defendant's answer. It denies everything accompanied by the counterclaim alleging that the plaintiff himself is guilty of breach of trust and fraud. The demand for punitive damages in the counterclaim doubles the plaintiff's demand in the complaint.

As the litigation proceeds it is interrupted by unsuccessful efforts at mediation. The mediators wind up telling the parties the obvious—you people must resolve the case because you will destroy each other if the litigation continues. This makes no impression on the litigants. I heard a frustrated mediator tell this story:

A scorpion on the bank of the Nile asks a frog to ferry him to the other side.

"Oh, no," the frog says, "you will kill me with your stinger."

"That's ridiculous," the scorpion says, "because then I would drown with you."

The logic is convincing. The frog takes the scorpion on his back and begins the swim across the river. In midstream the scorpion plunges his stinger into the frog's neck. The sinking frog groans, "Why, why, now we both shall die."

The scorpion shrugs and says: "Don't you know? That is the way we decide things around here."

In one mediation I attended, my client kept saying to the mediator that his former partner lied all the time and was a very good liar. The mediator asked: "A really good liar? You'd better settle. If he is as good as you say he is, he will be believed."

Appeals to rationality, anecdotes, and good sense do no good. Each former business partner says to the mediator in a private interview, "I know him so well. Any show of weakness, any sign of reasonableness, and that bully will take everything he can get."

The litigation goes forward and as it does it metastasizes from one *forum non conveniens* to another. It may start here in the District of Columbia as a divorce case and then draw in family members. If there are any family business entities, it may draw them in also. It is not unusual for the family business to include a Delaware corporation. That means that the Delaware courts are involved. It is not unusual for the litigation to spread to both of the adjoining counties of Maryland and Virginia. In time some of the cases go to trial and some are stayed. The courthouse file expands into separate volumes, often running into so many files that the clerks cannot keep them together. Every file contains abusive allegations, sanction motions, motions to seal the record, and occasionally an affidavit of prejudice supporting a motion to recuse the trial judge. Lawyers appear and disappear. Any lawyer who tries to talk sense to the combatants is discharged in favor of someone "who knows how to fight."

The above diagram is what we have where people with too much money who know a lot about each other engage in reciprocal meanness fueled by many years of observing each other's method of operation. It was all right when they were co-conspirators, but it is a fight to the death when they become enemies.

The question that arises is whether courts are obligated to put up with these aberrations of the litigious idle rich. Rule 1 of the Federal Rules of Civil Procedure says that the rules "shall be construed and administered to secure the just, speedy and inexpensive determination of every action." Such a rule requires the courts to be innovative in getting this nasty, time-consuming litigation out of the courts and onto a psychiatrist's couch. Nasty litigation produces delays that needlessly deprive legitimate litigants from getting a speedy, inexpensive determination of their cases.

Here is my suggestion. The court creates a DL calendar, DL standing for Disreputable Litigation. A case so identified as being a nasty case goes on the DL calendar. An experienced judge is assigned to meet with counsel for the combatants and advise them that the courts are not going to be held hostage.

The procedure for such DL cases allows only one deposition for each side, limited to two hours. Once the depositions are over, the case is assigned to an arbitrator for nonbinding arbitration. Each litigant is invited to describe to the arbitrator, privately and without interruption, the villainy of his or her adversary. This recitation shall identify the various blackmail elements in the case. These include fraudulent tax returns, documents destroyed, cash skimmed from the various business ventures, and the use of company funds to pay the rent of a love nest. Each is given a chance to unload each other's gun.

The nonbinding arbitration must be completed within 45 days after the answer and counterclaim are filed. If the case does not settle, it is set down for trial within the month. Each side is given no more than three days to present its case.

The lawyers, once the case is labeled DL, must now tell their clients that it will all be over in three months. If the parties are thinking of deposition after deposition of witnesses for and against, they must resign themselves to a quick ending. This is bad news for nasty litigants. How can you punish the other side if the case is over so quickly?

A lawyer who appears frequently in DL calendar cases will find that judges are appointing him to case after case to represent indefatigable but impecunious litigants who require the immediate attention of an overly aggressive lawyer.

THE CLIENT WHO PAYS
AND THE CLIENT WHO
DOES NOT

Y ou cannot practice law without them. You cannot establish independence in a law firm, these wonderful days, without a group of clients who will follow you from firm to firm as you bargain up.

There are two main categories of clients: the client who pays a reasonable bill when rendered and the client who does not. Those who pay and accompany it with a letter of thanks represent an endangered species.

The dominant species is the client who turns belligerent when the time comes to pay. He is all for litigation, no matter the cost until the computer clicks out the bill. Then all that the lawyer was encouraged to do to get at the adversary is called into question. Why so many depositions? Why so many motions? The terms of engagement now change. The lawyer is the adversary.

The ups and downs of the real estate market brought into existence another client type, the underfunded commercial litigator. He wants to litigate his deals for whatever advantages litigation produces. He wants to be in the game, so to speak. He sees the big players litigating each deal in order to get a better deal. It is he who thought up the concept of lender liability. No lawyer, on his own, would have the imagination to create a cause of action against a lender because the lender has the audacity to want to be paid as promised. The underfunded commercial litigator puts up just enough money to pay the retainer, the entrance fee. His lawyer files the original pleadings—the complaint or the answer and obligatory counterclaim.

A few discovery waves and the retainer is used up. By this time the lawyer and the client are litigation friends. They dine together and the client puts it on his credit card. They may take vacations together. The lawyer is in the process of being manipulated just the way the client manipulated those involved in the real estate deal that is the subject of the pending litigation.

What makes the arrangement particularly onerous for the lawyer is the client's rejection of the settlement offer that would provide a little money for the client and would pay the lawyer's bills. The client's strategy is to push the issue to the point where the lawyer begs the client to settle. The client then says, "But why should I settle? You get paid, but what is in it for me? Reduce your bill and we can do some business." The trap is sprung.

I have often wondered why it is that lawyers take on clients known within the profession to be slow-pay or no- pay. Perhaps the lawyer who signs on believes he can outfox the client. He is wrong. The client does not have to play by any rules. The lawyer does. The lawyer loses. Well, maybe not always. There is a story concerning Max Steuer, a leading New York trial lawyer in the 1920's and 1930's. He was involved in an arbitration hearing. He represented a client interested in overzealous representation and underpaid legal services. Steuer said not a word at the hearing until a white envelope passed from the client to Steuer's co-counsel, who made a count of the cash. When co-counsel nodded, Steuer announced he was ready.

The client I find interesting is the one who interviews lawyers before committing. He says his case is a sure thing. There are five lawyers bidding for the case. One letter and there will be a huge settlement. Experience has taught me to tell such a client that I do not accept sure things. I have never had a sure thing. I would not know how to deal with a sure thing. The client should consult a sure- thing specialist.

And what of the client who quivers with suspicion concerning everything and everybody? I enjoy spending time with such people, not because I wish to represent them but to study the symptoms of an incurable disorder. Such a person is hesitant to tell me the facts because I might have as a client the person he wishes to sue.

The wish to litigate, for some people, can be an obsession. Piero Calamandrei, in his book *Eulogy of Judges*, describes such a person:

> I know a venerable litigant, now more than ninety years old, who after the age of sixty brought a suit over a disputed inheritance. His adversaries, who were then young, thought the best tactics were to wear the old man out by dilatory methods in order to hasten his death, which they expected in the near future. Thus began an epic duel between civil procedure and longevity. As the years have passed generations of lawyers have defended the parties, and one by one the judges who handed down the early decisions have gone to their last rest.

The old gentleman, instead of aging, seems to take on new life from every procedural objection which further postpones the final decision.

I have met and represented the type. At heart he is a born gambler. Lawsuits and the lottery are his source of stimulation. Gambler that he is, he would rather lose a lawsuit than not to be in litigation at all. And there is always the appeal.

NEW BUSINESS

Ajudge of my acquaintance, a busy lawyer before he went on the bench, said what he missed most was that call about a new case. The expectation of new business, the belief that the best case is the next case, is the magneto in the mind of most of the interesting lawyers I have known. The belief that the next phone call may bring the magic that will change everything for the better is my understanding of legal optimism. J. B. Priestley speaks in an essay entitled "The Moments" of the magic moments, which for a lawyer often appear as new business:

> All my life, I now realize, I have been nourished and
> secretly sustained by certain moments that have always
> seemed to me to be magical. If I have completed the
> tasks and shouldered the burdens all the way, finishing
> the marches without handing over my rifle and pack or
> dropping out, it is neither conscience nor energy that
> has kept me going but the memory and the hope of

this magic. It has visited me before; it will come again. Sooner or later I would taste the honey-dew once more.

The magic may put to rest a brooding apprehension by the receipt of an order reinstating, *nunc pro tunc*, a case dismissed because of failure to prosecute. Reinstated and no statute of limitations problems! There's magic in the air.

I often recall a Faustian bargain I once made in a criminal case. I vowed to waive all entitlement to future magic moments, now and in perpetuity, if the jury would return a verdict of "not guilty." It did.

Have I kept that vow? Of course not. These things, as Priestley says, go beyond logic, fairness, and what we are entitled to. Even if one were to apply sound legal principles to such promises, it is hornbook law that vows made under emotional duress are rescindable at the option of the misrepresenter.

The magic I speak of is distinguishable from good luck. Good luck is beating the odds, hitting the jackpot. Magic transcends such bourgeois material considerations. It deals with more important things, such as an unexpected meeting that grows into a rewarding friendship. The practice of law offers many opportunities to develop a wide circle of friends. A joint defense agreement may create a bond that survives the conviction and sentencing of all defendants.

A most rewarding friendship began when I was retained to represent lawyers who wished to enforce a contract they claimed they had made with a prosecutor. Within the group was a lawyer well known for representing unpopular clients. He was displeased that I had been selected as counsel. Although he went along with it, he made a point of not speaking to me. One day as the court proceeding droned on we happened to be sitting next to each other. He said abruptly: "Do you understand that in the cases I am in there is a credible basis for indignation about the way the government treated my client? I specialize in the representation of the unjustly accused people whose rights have been violated." I said I was aware of this.

He then added: "And if any such indignation exists in the case we are now in, I have been unable to discover it." We both laughed, we became good friends. As we got to know each other I saw in him the lawyer I would have liked to have been.

Priestley says these moments arrive as and when they choose. They cannot be summoned at will. If they could, they would not have the unpredictability that makes them unique. But there are circumstances that we prospectors for the golden moment believe are propitious.

It is not a secret that many in the legal profession are dissatisfied with their work. They believe that what they do separates them from the music in life, and they are entirely correct in that belief. The marking up of pre-bills to make sure there is an over-realization of the hourly rate is not a circumstance to start one humming a Strauss waltz. Here is what I recommend:

Rent Charlie Chaplin's *The Gold Rush, Limelight,* and *Monsieur Verdoux.* Do not expect to be amused. Chaplin's comedy does not age well. What does survive, for those who have eyes to see, are smile-though-your-heart-is-aching scenes. It is my belief that an exposure to pathos brings a compassion for those that life has mistreated.

Before you know it, the world looks different. You have been lucky. The phone will ring. You will be retained in a real case by a real client who needs you and nobody else. You now have what all lawyers need, new business, the portable business required to declare your personal declaration of independence. You have had your magic moment.

As the years pass we deplete our entitlement. One day we realize no magic is left. Our ration is all used up. To know just when that is is to know just when to cancel the malpractice coverage and retire to a legal hospice.

POLITICIANS AS CLIENTS

T wo politicians were in their lawyer's office. Both were the subject of gossip that they received gifts from a questionable source. One of the politicians was reserved, dignified, and somewhat concerned that unfavorable inferences would be drawn concerning certain events. The other was garrulous.

The garrulous gentleman said: "I am sorry to say that if I told all I knew about this the top would fly off the United States Capitol."

The other said: "Well, if I look out my office window and see the top of the Capitol fly off, I will know you have given an interview."

A politician must be wary of keeping a diary. It is likely to be a source of embarrassment, or worse yet, evidence against the diarist. He also should not discuss his case with others who may be witnesses against him. A proescutor who wants to be spiteful will allege that this is an effort to affect a witness's testimony, or to put it another way, an obstruction of justice.

EVIDENCE

Some circumstantial evidence is very strong, as when you find a trout in the milk.

Henry David Thoreau

CIRCUMSTANTIAL EVIDENCE AND ARTIE SCHOPENHAUER

Martin Armstrong had obtained two continuances from the court to file his opposition to the defendant's motion for summary judgment.

He had a touch of the attention deficit disorder about the case. He could not bring himself to read the file. He knew he must go someplace where there would be no distractions. He decided to take the file and nothing else to that second rate hotel in Boston where he stayed in his student days.

When he got to the hotel, the clerk told him to leave his briefcase in the lobby and come back in an hour or two and his room would be ready. He decided he would kill time in the used bookstore in the neighborhood. But not to buy any books; that would distract him.

He went to the table where for a dollar one could pick up a stray volume from one of the multi-volume sets. He saw one of Arthur Schopenhauer's books, titled *Counsels and Maxims*. Despite his resolution to buy no books, he could not pass up this dollar bargain. He got acquainted with Schopenhauer in his philosophy class at Harvard. He liked the old boy's pessimism.

He felt guilty about breaking his resolution. But a page or two of Schopenhauer would not be a problem. He took a few turns around Bromfield Street, enjoying the pleasant fall weather, then returned to the hotel. His room was just what he wanted, a bed, a desk, a chair, a small closet. No radio. No TV. No distractions.

Now, once and for all, he was going to read the pleadings and the papers, no skipping. He soon realized that there was not much to the defendant's motion. Why had he been frightened by it?

After two hours of work he stood up, stretched himself, and looked around the small room. The cleaning people did a poor job. The last occupant was a smoker and a drinker. The ashtray was filled with cigarette butts. Beneath the bed was an empty half-pint whiskey bottle. He put both in the trash basket. He had been clean of smoking and drinking for three years. If he were to spend a week in this room, he might fall off the wagon.

He felt exhilarated after writing the first draft. He decided to take a walk, eat a sandwich, and return to the room. He said to himself that he had now earned the right to read a few of Schopenhauer's maxims including the advice that "to speak angrily to a person, to show your hatred by what you say or by the way you look is an unnecessary proceeding -- dangerous, foolish, ridiculous, and vulgar." Well, that is pretty good.

There was a one-page paper note in the back of the book. It was a suicide note, filled with despair and futility. It contained a Schopenhauer quotation:

> Life may be represented as a constant deceiver in things great and small. If it makes promises, it never keeps them, . . . Life gives only to take away. The charm of distance shows us a paradise which vanishes like an optical delusion if we allow ourselves to approach it.

Well, somebody in that state of mind should have not been reading Schopenhauer.

The Boston fall weather outside was pleasant. Martin Armstrong tried to open the window facing the street. It would not open. It had not been opened for some time. There were chipped coats of old paint around the window. He thought of those lead poisoning cases he had lost.

Armstrong placed himself where he could put all his strength behind the effort. The window did not open, but something else happened. He got a sharp chest pain. Why did he get all worked up about opening that window? His cardiologist had warned him against doing anything that involved real physical effort.

He breathed deeply but the pain did not go away. He looked through the leather pouch where he kept his shaving supplies to see if he had the prescription bottle of nitroglycerine pills. The bottle was there, but no pills. He did find his over the counter sleeping pills. In the past when he had sharp pains, he took a nitroglycerine pill together with the sleeping pill. If he got a good night's sleep the pain went away. He took two of the "bluies," the blue pills that guaranteed to give a good night's sleep, and if you don't believe it, just read the label.

The following morning the cleaning woman knocked on his door. No answer. She reported this to the desk clerk who, with the help of others, pried open the lock. Armstrong was in bed, dead. The police were called. The policeman found the suicide note. He then called the doctor whose name appeared on the empty nitroglycerine bottle.

The policeman identified himself and asked if the doctor had Martin Armstrong as a patient. The doctor confirmed that he did.

"Did you prescribe nitro pills for him?" The doctor said he did.

The policeman said, "What if he took a lot of pills and smoked a lot and drank a bottle of whiskey -- would that have any effect?" The doctor said that would be a real problem.

"Well, it looks like Martin Armstrong has died, and left a suicide note."

The doctor said, "Something must have gone wrong for Martin to end up like this. Something must have really gone wrong for him to be in the hotel you have described. Why wasn't he staying at the Ritz, his favorite hotel in Boston? Something must have really gone wrong."

HE SHOULD HAVE
LOOKED

The rule, which requires that all evidence which is introduced shall be relevant to the guilt or the innocence of the accused, is always applied with considerable strictness in criminal proceedings. The wisdom and justice of this, at least from the defendant's standpoint, are self-evident. The defendant can with fairness be expected to come into court prepared to meet the accusations contained in the indictment only, which in this case was the larceny of the Dodge automobile. On this account, all the evidence offered by the State should consist wholly of facts which were within the range and scope of the allegations contained in the indictment upon which he is being tried. The evidence introduced over the defendant's objection relating to other offenses than that charged in the indictment no doubt alarmed the suspicions of the jury, or at least it may have had that effect, and inclined them the more readily to believe in the guilt of the defendant of the offense charged.

Dennison v. State, 17 Ala. 674, 88 So. 211 (1921) (Bricken, J.)

(larceny of an automobile)

Does not that long paragraph say that it is unfair of the prosecutor to charge a defendant with one specific crime and then put in evidence of other crimes and bad acts unconnected with the specific crime? It is unfair because the prosecutor proves the general bad character of the defendant to show he is evil and therefore must be convicted, guilty or not.

Or try this even shorter summary: "Evidence of other crimes, wrongs, or acts is not admissible to prove the character of a person in order to show conformity therewith." That is the way the Federal Rules of Evidence state the principle. As John Mortimer's Horace Rumpole would say, this is the golden thread of fairness that runs through our criminal law.

If things ended there, Rumpole would be correct. The law would be as Judge Bricken gave it in 1921. But by the time the Federal Rules of Evidence came to us on the stone tablets, the law had changed.

The very next sentence of Rule 404(b) opens a wide door through which the forbidden evidence proudly enters the case. It says that the bad stuff may be admissible "for other purposes, such as proof of motive, opportunity, intent, preparation, plan, knowledge, identity, or absence of mistake or accident" or anything else a resourceful prosecutor can dream up.

Two authorities on the subject, professors Paul F. Rothstein and Edward J. Imwinkelried, declare that the irreconcilable conflict between these two sentences, the first forbidding the use of uncharged misconduct and the second inviting it, produces more litigation, law review articles, and commentary than any other evidentiary rule. Lexis turns up well over 3,000 hits.

Now let us go from the abstract to the specific. There was a middle-aged man who was attentive to young women. He repeatedly induced his young women friends to go on motoring trips from his home in Maine to Toronto, Canada. When he returned, he returned alone. The women were never seen again. The local police became suspicious. They obtained a search warrant and found in his apartment joint bank account books naming the missing women. He was indicted. He was charged in one count with the murder of just one of the women.

The prosecution offered evidence in three other cases involving women who disappeared. The defense lawyer predicted the trial judge would let in the evidence of the three other cases, the uncharged misconduct. When that evidence got before a jury, that would be the end of the case. He decided to go nonjury.

The judge did let in the prejudicial evidence, pointing out the compelling similarity in the cases. They showed the "signature" of the defendant. Each case was the same as the other. Each proved the other.

The lawyer in closing argument put the judge on the spot. He said the prosecution was trying to prove the case charged in the indictment by proving three other so-called similar cases. Accepting the judge's logic, if one of the girls was alive, the prosecutor's case must fail.

"Judge, if just one of those women enters the court, you must return a verdict of not guilty. That is the logical conclusion based on your similarity ruling."

The lawyer turned dramatically and pointed to the courtroom door. The judge's clerk stared at the door. So did the judge. So did the gallery.

Three minutes of silence. Nobody entered. Defense counsel turned and faced the judge and said, "I have demonstrated to you and your clerk that both of you have a reasonable doubt. If you were convinced beyond a reasonable doubt the women were murdered, why stare as you did with your eyes fixed at the door?"

Despite the argument, the judge found the defendant guilty.

"You made a good logical argument. I grant you that you may have created a reasonable doubt—except for one thing. You convinced everybody but your client. He looked straight ahead during the entire three minutes. Good argument—bad witness prep."

THE JUDGE

The function of the trial judge is to be quick, courteous, and wrong. That is not to say that the Court of Appeals should be slow, rude, and right, for that would usurp the function of the Supreme Court.

The Judge's Charge

The judge's charge was clear and plain,
It meant his side the suit should gain;
But hours he waited, and report
The jury none made to the court.
"Go, bring them in, and we will see
What may their trivial problem be;
Perhaps some technical word of art,
Or else some juror oversmart."
The bailiff went, filed in the array,
The judge the silence broke to say,
"A verdict, gentlemen, have you found?"
The foreman spoke, and somewhat frowned,
"Your Honor, we are eleven to one."
"And tell me, pray, who may he be.
Perhaps he does not clearly see.

The points the court made in its charge,
I may repeat them more at large."
"No," said the foreman, "naught can change
Him in his fixed opinion strange;
We've argued long, he takes a pride
In arguing always on your side."

John Augustus Wilstach

Judgeomania

"If men were horses, beggars would ride,"
And tramps become sailors, were wine in the tide;
And all would be changed if "if" we could clench,
So here's what I'd do,

        Were I on the bench.

The lawyers I'd greet with "How-do, old chap;
Yes, yes, I've forgotten that legal scrap;"
'Twixt bench and bar there's no wid'ning trench,
I'd treat all as friends,

        Were I on the bench.

I'd be gracious to all, so drop your reserve;
I'd talk so a man wouldn't lose all his nerve;
I'd award liberal fees—no cause to retrench;
There'd be money galore,

        Were I on the bench.

Res iner alios acta *(translated,*
Things between others were demonstrated);
I'd abolish all Latin, and also the French;
There'd be English alone,

        Were I on the bench.

If a case took two hours or longer to try
(For talking is bound to make a man dry),

82

A recess we'd take, our thirst we would quench;
I'd guard well your health,

                        Were I on the bench.

If counsel were young and apt to be beat,
I'd beckon him up to the judge's seat,
And give him advice so success he could wrench;
Nor, would you be happy

                        Were I on the bench.

I'd abolish opinions if made at great length,
They take up so much of a law student's strength;
Then law'd be a mistress and no ugly wench;
But all with this IF

                        Were I on the bench.

                               Harry A. Bloomberg

Contrasts in Court

This advocate, in confidence so weak
He scarce can muster breath enough to speak,
And gets each sentence by a painful wrench,
Wears in his hat more wit than half the Bench.

This other, self-assertive, shallow, loud,
Would still harangue his judges like a crowd,
Though Cicero himself were seated there
In full-robed splendor in his ivory chair.

                               Wendell P. Stafford

COURT REPORTERS

I write this during a deposition.

A lawyer's needless questioning of a deponent, which is what is going on now, is not anything new in deposition practice. What is new is deposition technology. The court reporter in this room has a computer wired to her stenotype machine. As she types shorthand, the computer converts the shorthand into a finished transcript that appears immediately on her computer screen and on the computer screens of the lawyers in the room.

The lawyers have in front of them, in addition to their computers, big, thick, heavy exhibit books filled with hundreds of tabbed documents. Depositions, these days, are about the exhibits, the e-mails, the memoranda, the drafts leading up to the final document, computer printouts, stock quotations, and medical records. Each question and answer turns on an exhibit marked by the court reporter and placed before the witness.

Wires running from wall sockets to the computers cover the floor. Walking around the room without tripping is for acrobats.

What would Lucius Friedli make of all this? Mr. Friedli was a court reporter. Mr. Friedli would not know what to make of all these wires, computers, and huge document books.

He prospered at a time when there were no computers and no stenotype keyboards. He took it all down in Pitman shorthand.

He prepared himself at the outset of the deposition by placing antique fountain pens, Parkers and Watermans, and straight pens side by side. Close by were his two ink bottles together with an eyedropper used to inject ink in the court reporter pens. Three wire-topped shorthand pads and clean cloths to be used to wipe the ink off the pens and off Mr. Friedli's fingers completed the preparation.

Mr. Friedli would then say, "Ready." Lawyers deferred to him. Mr. Friedli decided when the deposition commenced and when there would be a recess.

If the lawyers interrupted each other, he said, "One of you shut up. I cannot write with both hands." If the bickering continued despite the warning, Mr. Friedli threw down his pen. This brought civility.

The lawyers respected Mr. Friedli's judgment concerning witness credibility. If Mr. Friedli thought a witness was lying, he gave a skeptical look at the witness. Lawyers took note.

Mr. Friedli had sympathy for young lawyers. He gave them advice. I represented a defendant who was sued for defamation. The plaintiff claimed that my client, the defendant, called the plaintiff a liar in front of fellow employees and this adversely affected his reputation among those who heard it. I was deposing the plaintiff who in his answers repeated he was a person of good character. Mr. Friedli started shaking his head at these repetitious statements.

Mr. Friedli, after an hour of this, announced he needed a recess. He had the habit of walking the halls during a recess. As I walked past him, he said, "You are getting nowhere. Here is what you should do and let's get this over. Have him repeat one more time that everybody thinks he is an angel. Then say this: 'Mr. Plaintiff, your reputation is so good that none of the people who heard you called a liar believed a word of it.' He will say yes. That is the end of his case. When you have it, shut up and let's get this nonsense over with."

If a lawyer or a witness said something scurrilous, Mr. Friedli would ask, "Do you want me to put this in the transcript?"

This deposition going on right now, as I sit here, began with the usual ritual. The lawyer taking the deposition says the following, in one version or another, to the witness: "Mr. Witness, if I ask you a question that you do not understand, please tell me and I will do my best to clarify the question. I am interested in your recollection of what happened. I am not here to trick you or to trap you into a wrong answer. If you wish to take a break, you can do so at any time."

At a deposition I attended, the above speech was given to the witness. The lawyer, a cunning fellow, after putting the witness at ease with this statement, asked the witness a very tricky question. It was a question that summarized the witness's prior testimony so that the witness would give the answer the lawyer wanted rather than the answer the witness intended to give.

The witness's lawyer said to the witness, "Would you please leave the room?" Then he said to the lawyers asking the questions: "When this deposition started and you said to the witness you didn't intend to use any trick questions, the only person in this room (there were five lawyers in the room) who believed a word you said was the witness. The rest of us were just waiting for you to do what you do so well. Now, I am calling the witness back in the room and I invite you to apologize to him."

There was no apology, but the deposition ended quite abruptly.

CROSS-EXAMINATION

Cross-examination is beyond any doubt the greatest legal
engine ever invented for the discovery of truth.

John Henry Wigmore

Lawyer to witness: Do you drink?
Witness to lawyer: That's my business.
Lawyer to witness: And do you have any other business?

Court TV brings this great
legal engine right into the bedroom. Court TV also brings
instant commentary by the acknowledged experts on just how
the art should be practiced. The experts repeat the platitudes.
Never ask a question unless you know the answer. Always keep
control of the witness. Do not cross-examine without a purpose
and a plan to accomplish the purpose.

The first popular treatment of cross-examination was
Francis Wellman's *The Art of Cross-Examination*, originally published in 1903. It remains in print. Wellman gave examples of

dramatic cross-examinations as done by the turn-of-the-century leaders of the bar.

In Wellman's day cross-examination was conducted under circumstances very different from the cross-examinations we see today on TV. In those faraway times the examiner did not have the benefit of discovery—the full pretrial disclosure required under the present rules in both civil and criminal cases. Pretrial discovery brought on what is called the litigator. The litigator developed a specialty of perplexing and exhausting an opponent through the use of interrogatories, waves of depositions, requests for admissions, mental and physical examinations, and requests for sanctions. This type of litigation rarely involves a trial.

Wellman's cross-examiners operated on instinct and experience. Most of the time they did not know what a witness was going to say until the direct examination was concluded. The cross was prepared contemporaneously with the giving of the direct. The cross-examiner adapted the cross to the personality and demeanor of the witness on the stand. It was the interplay between the witness and the lawyer that determined whether the cross-examination was good or bad. There were always surprises.

Judge Jerome Frank in his book *Courts on Trial* tells this story to show how unpredictable a witness can be:

A trial judge who, after hearing the testimony and the lawyers' arguments, announced:

"Gentlemen, if Humphrey, the deceased, said—in the light of these Missouri decisions—'Daughter, if you'll come and live with me, I'll give you this house,' then I'll decide for the plaintiff. Now just what was the testimony?" Unfortunately the court reporter had boggled his notes. The judge impatiently asked if the principal witness, the plaintiff's maid, was present, and, learning that she was in the courtroom, asked her again to take the stand and repeat her testimony.

This is what she said:

"I remember very well what happened. It was a cold and stormy night. We were all sitting around the fire. Old Mr. Humphrey said to Mrs. Quinn, 'In the light of these Missouri decisions, daughter, if you'll come and live with me, I'll give you this house.'"

If you had to cross-examine that witness, the witness who just gave that testimony, would you ask her why she included the *Missouri* cases?

That "why" question—why did you do it, why didn't you do it?—is a seductive impulse. The TV authorities uniformly and strongly advise against asking the why question on cross-examination. The why question on cross gives the witness the opportunity for an open-ended answer.

Despite the conventional wisdom, I often ask the why question on cross-examination. In fact, it is my favorite question. An English judge, Henry Cecil, agrees with me. A why question, he says, opens up significant possibilities:

Although it may seem a simple thing to learn to ask why, it is of the greatest value both in the legal profession and in life generally. "Why?" and "Why not?" are two questions that every experienced advocate asks of his clients.

"Did you think that Mrs. Jones was sexually attractive?"

"Yes."

"Did you ever kiss her?"

91

"Yes."

"Did you ever commit adultery with her?"

"No."

"Did you ever ask her to commit adultery with you?"

"No."

"Why not?"

If no satisfactory answer could be given to that question, the probability is that at least one of the previous answers was a lie.

Every lawyer can recall—and never tires of—giving examples of his or her great skill at cross-examination. It so happens that great, really great, cross-examinations can lose a case. The witness under examination may be so cruelly chewed up that the overall effect is jury hatred directed at the lawyer and vicariously at the lawyer's client.

When I stand up to cross-examine I keep in mind Charlie Bellows, a leader of the Chicago criminal bar some years ago. Charlie had converted his mind into a reliable lie detector. When he caught a witness in a lie, as he often did, he made a show of compassion for the liar. A jury could well believe that Charlie genuinely regretted embarrassing the witness. Charlie also was master of the why question.

And when I dream I am conducting the great cross-examination. I am Gregory Peck in *The Paradine Case* or, better yet, Charles Laughton in *Witness for the Prosecution*. I am all-knowing, in control, using perfect language, all elegance and detachment, as I say, just as the English barristers do in the old movies, "I put it to you, sir ..." And then the dream ends as the witness puts it to me and another day in the office begins.

THE COURTHOUSE

This is that theater the muse loves best.
All dramas ever dreamed are acted here.
The roles are done in earnest, none in jest.
Hero and dupe and villain all appear.
Here falsehood skulks behind an honest mask.
And witless truth lets fall a saving word,
As the blind goddess tends her patient task
And in the hush the shears of fate are heard.
Here the slow-shod avengers keep their date;
Here innocence uncoils her snow-white bloom;
From here the untrapped swindle walks elate,
And stolid murder goes to meet his doom.
O stage more stark than ever Shakespeare knew.
What Peacock playhouse will contend with you?
Justice Wendell Phillips Stafford

F aded and yellowed with age, this poem, has had a place on my office wall for many years. How or when I came by it, I cannot recall. Until recently I knew nothing about its author. The other day an old bencher mentioned Stafford's name and it triggered some research.

Justice Stafford was a Vermonter born in 1861. He practiced law in Vermont and also served as a Vermont judge.

In 1904 President Theodore Roosevelt called Stafford to Washington and appointed him to the Supreme Court of the District of Columbia, where he served some 27 years. He threw his considerable energy behind prison reform and other worthwhile projects. In time he established an outstanding reputation as a judge.

He resigned in 1931 amidst great praise for his contribution to the court and to his adopted city. He died in 1953 at age 91.

Justice Stafford's court, although a federal district court, was the local court of general jurisdiction because of the District's odd legal status. Thus Stafford was the daily spectator where all dramas ever dreamed were acted. What did the lawyers who appeared before Stafford think of this man who wrote poetry about the courthouse?

I spoke with three lawyers who did appear in Stafford's court. George Monk and Ed Campbell recall Justice Stafford as a no-nonsense judge who ran a strict court. They recall a mustachioed man, of erect posture, dignified and reserved. Ed Campbell reminded me that justices became judges when the Supreme Court of the District of Columbia became the United States District Court.

Godfrey Munter recalls the judge as somewhat irascible with little patience for lawyers who drifted from the point or who were on the wrong side of the case.

The justice's published writings can be found in the law division of the Library of Congress. They consist of several books of poetry, an equity textbook, and a book of collected speeches. The speeches contain worthwhile reflections on law and lawyers.

The gifted lawyer for him was the lawyer with the power to perceive the true relations of things, a commonsense quality. "And who will not admit that common sense is always a gift of nature? If you know of any college that can confer an honest degree in common sense, let me know—I want to send my boy there."

The practice in Justice Stafford's day is revealed in his poetry and speeches. His cases involved human nature rather than large corporate or governmental interests. The lawyers who appeared before Stafford were specialists in the unraveling of secret human motivations. They eschewed the assembling of documentary evidence, the taking of discovery depositions, and the filing of Rule 11 motions. These were lawyers whose ambition it was to score a victory in a murder case, as Abraham Lincoln did with the use of the almanac and the phases of the moon.

How would Justice Stafford view the changes the years have brought to the practice of law? No doubt the growing impersonal nature of the practice would not be to his taste. A number of the changes were summarized by Thurman Arnold in his autobiography, *Fair Fights and Foul*. The practice of law, he wrote, was far more personal years ago. Big-firm law practice is an anonymous practice. The law offices resemble large corporate headquarters.

The chief asset of the big-city firm is the appearance it gives of institutional power rather than the personal reputations of its individual lawyers. There is no indispensable man or woman that the client seeks. As a partner gets a more lucrative opportunity, the partner persuades a less important client that some other member of the firm is just as qualified—or even more qualified—than he or she is. Legal talent is fungible. Any partner is presumed to be just as good as any other.

Stafford's poem came to mind again as I read an advertisement for the Courtroom Television Network. The ad announces that real live TV trials are on the way, "whether it's the LA cops or John Gotti on trial, or whether the issue is toxic torts or surrogate motherhood. TV brings the courtroom drama right into the home."

Justice Stafford, I feel certain, would have been repelled by the Courtroom Television Network. Litigants, as he saw them, were caught in a web of tragedy that often left permanent scars. Serve up these hapless victims as TV entertainment? Never.

LAWYERS

ADVICE TO A YOUNG LAWYER

Be brief, be pointed; let your matter stand
Lucid in order, solid, and at hand;
Spend not your words on trifles, but condense;
Strike with the mass of thought, not drops of sense;
Press to the close with vigor, once begun,
And leave (how hard the task!), leave off, when done.
Who draws a labored length of reasoning out,
Puts straws in line, for winds to whirl about;
Who drawls a tedious tale of learning o'er,
Counts but the sands on ocean's boundless shore.
Victory in law is gained, as battles fought,
Not by the numbers, but the forces brought.
What boots success in skirmish or in fray,
If rout and ruin following close the day?
What worth a hundred posts maintained with skill,
If these all held, the foe is victor still?
He who would win his cause, with power must frame
Points of support, and look with steady aim;
Attack the weak, defend the strong with art,
Strike but few blows, but strike them to the heart;
All scattered fires but end in smoke and noise,
The scorn of men, the idle play of boys.
Keep, then, this first great precept ever near,
Short be your speech, your matter strong, and clear,
Earnest your manner, warm and rich your style,
Severe in taste, yet full of grace the while;
So may you reach the loftiest heights of fame,
And leave, when life is past, a deathless name.

Whene'er you speak, remember every cause
Stands not on eloquence, but stands on laws;
Pregnant in matter, in expression brief,
Let every sentence stand in bold relief!
On trifling points, nor time, nor talents! waste,
A sad offense to learning and to taste;
Nor deal with pompous phrase; nor e'er suppose
Poetic flights belong to reasoning prose.
Loose declamation may deceive the crowd,
And seem more striking as it grows more loud;
But sober sense rejects it with disdain,
As naught but empty noise, and weak as vain.
The froth of words, the school-boy's vain parade
Of books and cases, — all his stock in trade, —
The pert conceits, the cunning tricks and play
Of low attorneys, strung in long array, —
The unseemly jest, the petulant reply,
That chatters on, and cares not how or why,
Studious, avoid unworthy themes to scan,
They sink the Speaker and disgrace the Man.
Like the false lights, by flying shadows cast,
Scarce seen when present, and forgot when past.

Begin with dignity; expound with grace,
Each ground of reasoning in its time and place;
Let order reign throughout, each topic touch,
Nor urge its power too little or too much.
Give each strong thought its most attractive view,
In diction clear, and yet severely true.
And, as the arguments in splendor grow,

Let each reflect its light on all below.
When to the close arrived, make no delays
By petty flourishes or verbal plays,
But sum the whole in one deep, solemn strain,
Like a strong current hastening to the main.

You wish the Court to hear, and listen too?
Then speak with point, be brief, be close, be true.
Cite well your cases; let them be in point;
Not learned rubbish, dark, and out of joint; —
And be your reasoning clear, and closely made,
Free from false taste, and verbiage, and parade.

Stuff not your speech with every sort of law,
Give us the grain, and throw away the straw.

Books should be read; but if you can't digest,
The same's the surfeit, take the worst or best.

Clear heads, sound hearts, full minds, with point may speak,
All else how poor in fact, in law how weak.

Who's a great lawyer? He who aims to say
The least his cause requires, not all he may.

Greatness ne'er grew from soils of spongy mold,
All on the surface dry; beneath all cold;
The generous plant from rich and deep must rise,
And gather vigor, as it seeks the skies.

Whoe'er in law desires to win his cause,
Must speak with point, not measure out " wise saws,"
Must make his learning apt, his reasoning clear,
Pregnant in matter, but in style severe;
But never drawl, nor spin the thread so fine,
That all becomes an evanescent line.

Joseph Story

A TRANSCENDENTAL
STATE

Last week I attended a meeting at a New York law firm that is the envy of the profession. The waiting room, if such an elegant room can be so identified, is what Louis Auchincloss had in mind when he wrote of the dignified, powerful Wall Street law firms. Everything is in quiet, understated good taste. The receptionist directed me across a well-worn Oriental rug to a leather club chair. On the way I passed a John Singer Sargent watercolor.

There was in the room a distinctive upper-class aroma. Joseph Alsop has described it as the aroma of the homes of old wealth. "I believe the secret was beeswax, rather lavishly used year-round to polish floors and furniture, plus a great many flowers from the summer gardens."

There were brochures on the table next to my chair. Inside the brochure was a brief history of the firm going back to the late nineteenth century. Then, to my astonishment, I saw a listing of recent cases the firm had won in the courts. Here was the proof, if proof were needed, that in these times all law firms must meet the competition the old-fashioned way, by shouting out how great they are. They must shout loudly enough to be heard by the general counsel of an oligopolist. A general counsel shopping for legal services can put a firm on easy street.

Nothing can be left to chance in such matters, and if it is advertisement that is required, then advertisement it shall be. Keep repeating how great it is to be great, how many big cases have been won, and how many honors have been collected.

And now let me tell you of a strange experience that is related to the New York experience. After returning to Washington, I was to meet with a prospective client. In such a meeting I would be doing in my way what the New York firm did in its brochure. I would be looking for openings to refer to cases won, books written, important people who might be called upon, my comprehensive knowledge of the relevant procedure, and a general capacity for omniscience. But none of that happened.

In the meeting I found myself in an out-of-body state. I had no desire to tell the shopper all of the cases I had won. I had no desire to drop names or give a learned discourse on jury behavior, pretrial pleading and practice, trick shots, and the idiosyncrasies of the innumerable judges I have known. I did not care if another lawyer got the case and made a front-page fortune. For these few minutes I was enjoying the bliss of the uncompetitive. I was in the land of the Tao, free from the anxieties and envy that disturb even those at the very top of the slippery pole.

As I sat there in awe of my own serenity, the shopper asked the inevitable question. "If I were to hire you, what would you sue for?" That question always makes me uneasy.

Serenity brought the appropriate answer. "Your suit must be filed in conformity with the Federal Rules of Civil Procedure. The rules require that the facts of your case are to be set forth in a short, plain statement. The amount you sue for is not a fact related to your claim." The shopper was puzzled by this short, plain statement. He said he had three more lawyers on his list he must see before making a decision. He said he doubted whether he would entrust his case to a lawyer who did not know how much to sue for. He added that the case was a sure thing, that it was just a question of how much. Even that remark caused no annoyance. The real me would have said, "I am not a sure-thing lawyer. Sure-thing law is a specialty. You should see a sure-thing specialist." The other me did not make that sarcastic remark. The other me thanked the shopper for the concision with which he stated his case.

I believe there is a connection between my visit to the New York law firm and the transcendental experience I just described. Lawyerly self-promotion, once commenced, is a full-time job. It requires eternal vigilance to see who is getting ahead. I did not appreciate the full burden of it until I had this moment of release. I can compare it to having a slight headache every day. We learn to tolerate it. We forget how wonderful it is to be without it.

Here let me speak through Sidney J. Harris. "On the pulley system, we go up when someone else goes down, and we go down when someone else goes up. We have no inner stability, because our emotional position keeps shifting in relation to the outside world." Harris goes on to say that most of us judge ourselves on a false relativistic basis. "If we meet someone richer, we feel poor, someone handsomer, we feel ugly, someone more fluent, we feel tongue-tied. If they are up, we are down."

My wonderful experience gave me a glimpse into a state reserved for the few who reach a professional maturity that frees them from the judgmental. I wish I knew the mantra that triggers a return of the bliss that transcends all other joys.

AN EMBARRASSMENT
OF ETHICS

Tacked to my office wall is an ecumenical Christmas card I received long ago. It bears the legend "What is hateful to thee, do not do unto others: that is the whole Law—all the rest is commentary." It has the virtue of simplicity and certainty.

Rule 1 of the Federal Rules of Civil Procedure states that the rules "shall be construed and administered to secure the just, speedy, and inexpensive determination of every action." Wright and Miller's explanation of the rules, at last check, fills twenty-eight volumes and *Moore's Federal Practice*, thirty-six volumes. If the author of Rule One were to pay us a visit, she might say Rule One was a good idea—it's a shame nobody tried it. Everything has become commentary.

Ethics, legal ethics in particular, has taken its own place within the commentary industry. To keep abreast of the subject, one must have the *ABA/BNA Lawyers' Manual on Professional Conduct*, the Model Code, and the Rules. In addition, keep at hand *The Law of Lawyering*, two volumes, by Hazard and Hodes. Then there are the opinions of one's own local ethics rules committee and one's local bar counsel.

There are legal ethics experts getting fees in the $500-an-hour range for sage comments on the commentary of legal ethics.

We have been pushed to the point where a competent and reasonably thoughtful lawyer is uncertain of his or her own understanding of what is right and wrong. The commentary in the law of ethics gives great power to the enforcer. In the case of legal ethics, the enforcer is whoever happens to be the local bar counsel.

Most bar counsel prosecutions begin with a client's complaint. The client who most frequently complains is the individual of small means who brought an insoluble problem to a sole or small-firm practitioner. The client would have liked to hire an established firm. But the client must settle for a lawyer willing to work for low wages. Thus the commencement of the relationship has within it the client's suspicion that he settled for a second-rater. The fact that the lawyer did not perform magic confirms the client's belief that his lawyer "messed up the case." The client complains to bar counsel. Experts, whose full-time occupation is the complex field of legal ethics, evaluate it. Experts are resourceful in finding violations that would not occur to nonspecialists.

A sole or small-office practitioner is not practicing in the same solar system as the well-funded firms with their computers, paralegals, checkers, double-checkers, and the final check. Nevertheless, the rules are enforced as if all lawyers have the means to check and double-check.

The practice of law at its most profitable involves sumo wrestling, for big fees and high stakes. Rarely does a Fortune

500 client complain to bar counsel. No complaints from Ford and Chrysler that outside counsel won't return phone calls. The big boys can take care of themselves. Therefore bar counsel must exercise its expertise on the lawyers who represent individuals who want more from the system than the system can give.

Perhaps the time has come to tell the lawyers who cannot afford oversight committees and computerized internal conflict checks that the law practice is not for them. If they practice without such apparatus, the odds are high that there will be complaints followed by letters from bar counsel.

From time to time the public is informed that the ethics industry demonstrates that the profession is policing itself. These public pronouncements and statistics are used as a cover by a profession at war with itself. It wants the rules of the marketplace for some. But it insists on strict compliance with the ethical rules for those trying to represent individuals who seek out a lawyer who charges $50 an hour rather than $500 an hour. Such lawyers are trying to perform a valuable service for a needy clientele. Much of what they do is *pro bono*. Occasionally they correct an injustice that, but for them, would remain unchallenged. I can say from personal knowledge that many of these plucky lawyers are threatened with or have been sanctioned where their culpability, if there was any, was technical and required an expert to explain the violation.

Is there a solution to the problems? I offer two. First, a halt on the prosecution of lawyers who, through inadvertence, may be in technical violation of one of the codes, rules, or annotations of the codes or rules or ethics opinions. And there must be a cap on funding bar counsel. As long as a prosecutorial office can get the funds, it finds cases. Many times a so-called case happens in such a manner that it is not of much consequence to the public whether it is pursued or not. Bar counsel's expertise and energy should be applied to real cases where there is real injury.

My second suggestion is that the ethics rules be restated to deal with the reality of the sole practitioner and the small-firm practice. I favor a simple preliminary statement. Call it Rule One:

> These rules shall be construed and administered to secure the just and reasonable enforcement of a lawyer's obligations leavened by a consideration of the burdens on the lawyer, the occasional mendacious paranoia of the complainant, and the occasional overzealousness of those "drest in a little brief authority."

BOTTLED WATER

It is September 1975. I am attending the deposition of a plaintiff who has sued five accountants. He claims they defrauded him. Each defendant is represented by a lawyer provided by his insurance company and each has his own personal lawyer. The room is filled with lawyers. Each lawyer is set up with a yellow pad with the questions to be asked of the plaintiff. To the right of the pad are two packs of cigarettes. To the left of the pad is a bottle of Coca-Cola. Ashtrays everywhere. The caffeine and the nicotine contribute to the undisciplined jocularity.

The plaintiff smokes contraband Cuban cigars. After a roll of his dental castanets, he bites off the end of the Montecristo Grande. He lights up. He takes a few puffs that produce the full atomic mushroom cloud between him and the lawyer asking the questions. It is apparent the witness believes he can outsmoke anybody in the room.

Before the witness answers a question, he pauses dramatically. He then gives his answer. "I do not recall." He is proud of the answer. He looks around the room to see how his response is received. His audience is unimpressed. As the deposition goes on, the witness demonstrates impressive resources of evasion to counter the slippery questions of the battery of lawyers. In other words, it was a well-done, good-old-boys deposition.

Now things have changed. All cases are now document cases. Each lawyer has a stack of documents. There are briefcases on the floor with yet more documents. Each question connects with a document. Each lawyer has two or more sherpas assisting in the climb. Each lawyer has his own computer. It is connected to the court reporter's computer. As the court reporter writes up the testimony, it appears at the same time on each lawyer's screen. It is all business. Nobody is smoking. There are no ashtrays. Yes, there are Cokes, but they are in cans. In addition there is bottled water everywhere.

I first saw bottled water in The Stafford Hotel in London. The label designated the contents as mineral water taken from some mountain spring known for its medicinal value. J. B. Priestley in one of his essays describes such water: "It will have been awarded gold medals and diplomas. It will attempt to cure rheumatism, catarrh of the stomach, urinary complaints, obesity and gout, gravel and stone."

Coca-Cola originated in the South and became the South's own mineral water. It claimed its secret formula had therapeutic value. It cured infants of upset stomachs and strong men of the blues.

A. J. Liebling was sent down south to write a hostile article about Huey Long's brother, Governor Earl Long of Louisiana. Earl Long converted Liebling to a believer. In Liebling's book about the governor he describes Long's use of Coca-Cola to protect him from an attack of heat exposure during a long, rambling stump speech. Governor Long paused and dipped his handkerchief in Coca-Cola and applied it to his brow. It brought immediate relief.

The switch from bottled Coke to Coke in cans must be noted. When Coke was sold in bottles, anyone who claimed competence as a personal injury lawyer had to be able to say he had tried a Coca-Cola exploding bottle case.

The theory of such a case is wrapped up in the doctrine of res ipsa loquitur ("the thing speaks for itself"). Here is a typical res ipsa jury instruction:

> Ordinarily, the fact that an accident happens does not mean it was caused by negligence. However, if each of the following circumstances is more probable than not, you may conclude that there was negligence: first, the Coke bottle would not ordinarily explode without negligence; second, the cause of the event was within the defendant Coca-Cola's exclusive control; third, no action by anyone else, including the plaintiff, was a cause of the explosion.
>
> Should you find that it is more probable than not that Coca-Cola was negligent, Coca-Cola is then called upon for a satisfactory explanation and may explain to your satisfaction that there was no negligence on its part which was a cause of the explosion.
>
> If you are not satisfied with Coca-Cola's explanation, then your verdict should be for the plaintiff.

Coca-Cola had trouble with exploding bottle cases. An exploding glass bottle causes serious injury. When I tried my first exploding bottle case, I used a closing argument the other plaintiff's lawyers had perfected. Here is a part of it:

> I wish this little bottle could talk (holding up the bottle for the jury to see). Do you know what it would say? It would say, "Ladies and gentlemen of the jury, Coca-Cola didn't give me a strong body. You couldn't tell by looking at me that I was defective. One side of me was not as strong as the other. They let me go to the store. I knew I might hurt somebody. Every place I went I was dropped, kicked, and suffered because of the way I was treated. Mr. Jones, the plaintiff, was a very nice fellow. He didn't mishandle me at all. I knew I couldn't hold together. I made a lot of noise and went to pieces, and here I am in Mr. Jones' jaw. I wish they could take me back and give me a new life and give him a new jaw."

Such poetic eloquence is out of style today. Real litigators look down on it. But in its time it gave one a feeling of having participated as a player in the high drama of the courtroom.

CONFESSING ERROR

The cunning behind a confession of error is summarized by La Rochefoucauld: "We confess little faults in order to suggest that we have no big ones."

The confession of error must be used sparingly. Though good for the soul, if done repeatedly, it is bad for the reputation.

When error is confessed with the proper attention to ritual, it is a pleasure to behold. The voice drops. The advocate leans forward. He places his hands on the sides of the rostrum. His face takes on the appearance of a ten-page affidavit. Of course, it is much easier for one of the older members of the bar to perform this rite because he can supply the suitable preamble, which is: "In my forty years at the bar, I have never found myself to be obligated to do what I am doing today."

The next part of the confession is the factual statement:
Your Honors, in the court below I was in error when
I persuaded the learned trial judge to rule that it was
a correct interpretation of the law to allow me to

personally enter the jury room and deliver the exhibits which the jurors asked for, and to give them an *ex parte* explanation of each exhibit. I might say in mitigation that I have found a Texas case, directly in point, which supports the procedure I followed, however, I am not asking Your Honors to follow that Texas case, although the trial judge was impressed with its reasonableness. After due reflection I confess that this was error. It was harmless error, but it was error.

If the theory of the attorney confessing error is correct, the appellate opinion will read as follows:

During oral argument the attorney for the plaintiff, in response to a question from the court, stated with commendable candor that it was error for the trial court to allow plaintiff's attorney to personally deliver the exhibits to the jury. It is indeed unfortunate that the trial judge permitted this to happen and also permitted the plaintiff's attorney to discuss with the jury these exhibits outside the presence of opposing counsel and the court. It might be added that the trial judge was persuaded to allow this procedure to occur after reading the persuasive language in the Texas case cited in the footnote. Although this court does not approve of the procedure, it does affirm the jury's verdict because the error was not prejudicial. This view is reinforced by the fact that the plaintiff's attorney, again with commendable candor, stated that he merely repeated to the jury his closing argument. Since the jury heard it once it certainly could not be harmed by hearing it again.

The plaintiff's attorney also promised, with his usual commendable candor, that he would not do this again nor would he cite the persuasive Texas case to any other trial court.

When proper ritual is not followed, the confessor may find that he has placed himself, without defenses, at the mercy of a vindictive tribunal. The line between success and failure is narrow.

CONVERSATION

What must one do to be a really bad conversationalist? What are the ways of the monstrous bore? The answers to these questions and others are found in a little book titled, *An Essay on Conversation*, written by H. W. Taft and published in 1927. Taft was a lawyer like his older brother, President William Howard Taft. Although Henry served with distinction as the grand master of the Wine and Food Society and as president of the Bar of the City of New York, his contemporaries found him a bit stuffy.

Taft mourns the death of the gentle art. After the obsequies, he says that the best conversations took place at long-ago English dinner parties and in the eighteenth-century French salons. A dinner party of six or eight composed of people of breeding, people with the common decency to be of fine parentage, offers the best contemporary opportunity for good conversation.

Mr. Taft devoted little in his essay to the conversation of his fellow lawyers, who, by profession, have certain advantages over others. Lawyers pick up gossip and inside information from their clients, bits and pieces of which create interest. This is offset by a lawyer's compulsion to talk about the cases he won, his brilliant cross-examinations.

The older a lawyer gets, the more cases he has won. Nevertheless, the conversation of lawyers is better than that of members of the other professions. Lawyers know the ways of the world and have had experience with the most interesting things life can offer, the study of human nature.

The worst time for lawyers to converse is the time spent waiting for the return of the jury. Each is constantly alert to the tap on the door. Most of the nervous energy is diverted into criticism of the trial judge. Why did he take two hours to instruct the jury on a simple contract issue? Why did he adjourn at two o'clock on Tuesday when there were five witnesses waiting to testify? If the jury is out for over an hour, every defect and weakness in the judge's personality has been explored.

After fully denouncing the judge, each lawyer then compliments his opponent, thereby seeking to get some reassurance for himself. Lawyers need flattery. In large doses, flattery can make an impending bad verdict tolerable.

THE STATUTE IS RUNNING

There is a tide in the affairs of litigation that meeting the deadlines, leads on to fortune; omitted, it ends with a letter from bar counsel.

Do you predate your calendar so that you are alerted three months before the crucial date? Do you stamp the outside of the files with the crucial date? Do you review your files on a Saturday morning?

No matter because at 3 a.m. you awaken with your heart pounding. You are certain that you permitted the statute to run in the case of *Doe v. Roe*. You sleep no more. You wonder if you also permitted a lapse of the malpractice policy. You indulge in fantasy confrontations with poor Mrs. Doe in which she said she meant to call and tell you not to go forward with her case. At dawn you stealthily leave your home and arrive at the office two hours earlier than usual.

You go to the file cabinet to get the Doe file. It has a way of slipping down in the drawer and disappearing from sight. You pull it up and out of the cabinet. Then, in the seconds it takes to look at the notes on the envelopes to determine if the three years have run, you make the resolutions that will protect you from such torture in the future.

Luckily for you the dates indicate that the statute will not run for another six months. You sigh and say to yourself you are still one of those for whom fortune has a smile.

Later in the day you announce that certain office procedures are going into effect. All files must be marked with the statute of limitations, and furthermore… On the way home that evening you may even meditate about the fact that everything should be done with dispatch. He who will not when he may, may not when he will.

Let us take an actual case. A lawyer is presented with a simple intersection collision. He should draw up a suit and make a claim for the property damage. The entire task would take twenty minutes if he gave it his full attention. It is so simple, so vulnerable, that it is put off because it can be done at any time. Once put off, however, time changes that innocuous file into an organism that has a disposition of its own bent on remaining unresolved. The victory of the file is achieved if it remains unfiled up to and including the time for the running of the statute of limitations.

Once the statute has run, the lethargy vanishes. He frantically consults the annotations dealing with factors that suspend the running of the statute. A reading of these annotations tells us of the unbelievable ingenuity of the lawyer trying to find a way out.

THE EXPERT WITNESS

Today's bar publications carry stories about lawyers who leave the profession. They assign a variety of reasons for leaving. These include the time demands, the incivility of the trial practice, and the feeling that the law practice is not what they thought it would be.

Years ago, when a lawyer left the practice he felt guilty about calling it quits. Even if he was spending most of his time in business ventures, he wanted people to think of him more as a professional rather than as a businessman.

The real estate bubbles seduce the best of lawyers. Buy low and sell high and make a million. Inside every lawyer representing a real estate speculator is a real estate speculator struggling to get out.

Let me tell you the story of a good lawyer with a good practice who took the bait. We will call him Richard Roe. He had a client who jumped from one successful real estate deal to another. Roe decided to put his expertise together with his client's talent for making money. They would make money beyond the dreams of avarice. One of their schemes was to get investors to put up money for Roe and Doe, Inc. to buy land, develop it, and then sell it at a great profit. Roe's partner spent weeks preparing the brochures depicting attractive homes in gated communities. These were distributed to the investors.

If Roe had not been inebriated with the exuberance of his own enthusiasm, he would have seen that these brochures would be the key exhibits in the lawsuits that would be filed (and were filed) by the investors who lost their money when the bubble burst.

Inevitably Roe and his partner had a falling out. Lawsuits followed. Roe's partner left all the problems to Roe. After all, Roe was a lawyer and the lawsuits fell within Roe's specialty. Roe finally decided he had enough. He tried to rebuild his law practice. It did not work. He ended his career defending the lawsuits and recalling the happy times when he was all lawyer.

A businessman does not read the fine-print transactional documents that lawyers prepare for him to sign. If he studied the details, the deal would go to someone else. He has in mind some tricky advantage often based on secret knowledge. He takes his chances. He has been lucky in the past relying on his intuition and he will be lucky again.

The skills of a trial lawyer, which is what Roe had, were of little value. He was fluent, logical, and analytical. He was trained to give reasons to explain what he did. None of this gave him an edge in dealing with people who, if asked to explain the reasons for their success, would mumble a few platitudes.

Roe said his bad experience had given him a great respect for those who thrive in a predatory culture. He understood it better because he did not have it. Those who do have it are quivering with the quick pulse of gain. They are good at quick mental arithmetic. They see a pecuniary advantage that others are blind to, and they are happiest when they boldly act on the opportunity. They don't question the irrational tax laws and the mysteries of depreciation. They exploit them.

They would rather gamble with other people's money than their own. The headline brokerage houses advertise that they know how to make others rich. There is contradiction here. Why would they want to give up their secrets?

Roe said there are exceptions. A good lawyer may find his way to the top of a stable business that has outgrown the need to take great risks. In such a business the conservative approach works well.

A friend who had a good practice was enticed into a 1970s real estate deal that did make him wealthy. Despite the fact that he had all the money he would ever need, he continued to maintain his law office. He wanted to be known as a lawyer, a member of an honorable profession.

I visited Joe at Sibley Hospital during his last illness. On one of the visits Dr. A was being paged. Dr. A appeared in court frequently as an expert witness in personal injury cases. I knew it would cheer Joe up if Dr. A came to his room and made believe that he knew Joe from around the courts. Dr. A agreed to do so. He came to Joe's room and said, "Joe, I recall you from the cases you tried around the courthouse. You were a pretty good lawyer." Joe responded to these flattering words with a warm smile. Joe said he had been ill and he had decided to retire from the law practice.

He said to Dr. A, "Do you still appear in court as much as you used to?" Dr. A said he had reached the point where he needed a fixed, unalterable deadline to motivate him to read the file before he testified. Therefore he only appeared in court if he was testifying before a senior judge.

Joe asked why Dr. A would only appear before a senior judge. Dr. A said, "Joe, it's this way. At my age, as I said, I need that pressing deadline to compel me to read the documents in the case. I know it will take 20 minutes for me to testify about all my qualifications, where I went to school, where I trained, where I have lectured, my board certifications, you know, all of that gold braid. As I said, that takes about 20 minutes. I have learned that a senior judge must take a 10-minute recess every 20 minutes. During that 10- minute recess I use the deadline to read the file. When the judge takes the bench, I am still one of the best around."

We left Joe's room. I thanked Dr. A for cheering up Joe. Dr. A said, "You know there's not a word of truth in that story, so don't repeat it."

DID YOU READ THE LATEST OPINION OF THE SUPREME COURT?

1. I read about it in *The New York Times*.
2. I saw the summary in *The Washington Post*.
3. I glanced through it.
4. I read the headnotes, or was it the syllabus?
5. I read about it in the newsletter we send to clients.
6. I will try and read it when I get back to the office.
7. Let's just say I flipped through it.
8. I liked that strong language in the dissent.
9. Where can I get hold of it?
10. Can you lend me your copy?
11. Is it filled with original intent?
12. I know roughly what it is about, but that's about it.
13. I haven't read it, but I spoke to one of the lawyers who was on the briefs.
14. I tried reading it but I couldn't get through it. Too much self-justification, too long.
15. I heard it discussed on Jim Lehrer's show.
16. I heard some of the oral arguments on C-SPAN Radio.
17. I usually take it to bed with me. It must be under the covers.

18. Congress will take care of it, just you wait and see.

19. Was it another punitive damages case, or was it the gun case?

20. I saw right away it had nothing to do with my clients, so I put it aside.

21. I never thought the Court would grant cert, and now I know it should not have.

22. After flipping through it, I think there ought to be two Supreme Courts: one to decide the legal issues, and another to decide the politics.

23. I put it all in my briefcase and read it on the subway.

24. I did read it, but I cannot recall the facts.

25. I saw the lawyers interviewed on the steps of the courthouse. One of them, I cannot recall his name, was sure he won.

26. 1 was hoping they would cite my law review article, but they didn't.

27. I read it, but I still cannot tell whether or not the sentencing guidelines are constitutional.

28. I was consulted about the case, but they went to somebody else after I said it might be a loser. I won't do that again.

29. A partner of mine was at the court when it was argued. He said he thought it would go the other way.

30. Why don't they televise the arguments?

31. Didn't the Chief Justice use the word *Kafkaesque* in one of his previous opinions? This recent opinion fits right in.

32. I attended the Georgetown Law Center's Supreme Court Institute Moot Court Program, and they predicted it.

33. To understand it, to really read it all, you would have to take off a day. I just don't have the time anymore.

34. Much of it was predictable.

35. I thought the court confused rather than clarified the issue. One of the dissents said just that.

36. How much of these opinions do the clerks write?

37. I am going into the hospital for minor surgery. I will read it there.

GOOD COUNSEL

There was a time when a lawyer's calling card carried the words *Attorney* and *Counsellor at Law*. I don't see the word *counsellor* any more. Perhaps it's too old-fashioned. The lithograph of the lawyer in the cluttered office, leaning forward to counsel the poor widow, is an anachronism. Today's law office is computer-driven. Little time is available for a leisurely conversation counseling the lonely and the desperate who cannot seem to get to the point.

Nevertheless, giving good counsel to someone with a serious legal problem is rewarding. And if the advice quickly solves the client's problem, it is good for the client and even better for the counsellor. It restores one's belief in one's self to know one knew the right answer. It does not happen often. But if it did happen once, it may happen again. Today's legal problems arrive within a tangled web of complexity that often defies a quick and clever solution.

There are lawyers gifted not so much in knowing what advice to give but in knowing how and when to give advice. These are the procedural skills that often determine whether the client acts on the advice that is given. Giving advice that is not taken discredits the advice giver.

I have studied talented counsellors at law in action. Let me summarize my observations for comparison with yours.

First and foremost, speak last. The person who speaks last has seen the clever ideas tested by those who have already spoken. Even though you may know the answer to the problem at the outset of the discussion, let others speak. Certainty held in reserve is beautiful to behold.

It is unwise to try to establish a reputation for always giving good advice. One bad guess and your reputation has suffered. Those with experience look for ways to avoid giving advice. One way is to state questions, not answers. "Yes, what Helen said sounds good, but what about that April 15th letter?" A clarifying question is better than a clever answer to the wrong question.

Another method is to select from the opinions of others but with a slight qualification. "Yes, Harry is right on that, but we must keep an eye on what others will do."

In a discussion of what to do, there are those who favor doing nothing. Better to wait and see what happens. Many problems solve themselves. Then there are those who want action. Any action is better than doing nothing. I have known cases where action, any action, is a mistake. Watergate was such a case. Watergate was a series of events and disclosures crisscrossing and working against one another. No one could identify the organizing design or grid. Every action was a blunder contributing to a larger blunder. The question to be directed to those who want action is, Will what you propose make things worse if it fails?

Best not to be dogmatic when giving advice. Do not suggest that you consider it a personal affront if your advice is rejected. Better to add the comment that there are things in what you say that must be looked at carefully.

In giving counsel there are those who rely on their broad knowledge of human nature. Such people are interested in personalities, why people act the way they do. They analyze the hidden motives that explain the events at hand: ego, sex, and the desire for power. They add gossip, cynical wisdom, and sarcasm concerning the character flaws of the opposition. Such talk has little to do with the facts of the case and the law. Most of it is likely to be a waste of time. It distracts us from the facts and the law.

Hungry people get nasty and mean-spirited. Lunch and dinner restore normality. Even the severely moral and the censoriously ascetic cannot forget food for more than three or four hours. The Chinese philosopher Lin Yutang says that our most constant thought every few hours is, When do I eat?

> International conferences, in the midst of discussion of the most absorbing and most critical political situations, have to break up for the noon meal. Parliaments have to adjust their schedule of sessions to meal hours. A coronation ceremony that lasts more than five or six hours or conflicts with the midday meal will be immediately denounced as a public nuisance.

Again from Lin:

> We rather hesitate to review unfavorably a book written by somebody who gave us a good dinner three

or four months ago. It is for this reason that, with the Chinese deep insight into human nature, all quarrels and disputes are settled at dinner tables instead of at the court of justice.

The food is now being wheeled into the conference room. Look at the pasta salad, the ham and turkey sandwiches, and those chocolate chip cookies as big as sewer tops. A slice of pound cake and a cappuccino and I discover how reasonable everyone is.

GOOD JUDGMENT

Asure way to destroy a lawyer's practice is to spread the rumor that he or she has bad judgment. On the other hand, a lawyer with a reputation for good judgment always gets clients. This raises a number of questions: What is good judgment? Is it a matter of experience? Is it an art form? Is it an instinct? Or is it all three?

Let me submit the platitudes concerning lawyer-like good judgment. A lawyer with good judgment does not prescribe a course of action that makes matters worse. A lawyer with good judgment does not undertake costly procedures that produce negligible gains.

A lawyer with good judgment perceives obvious traps to be avoided. A lawyer with good judgment determines what is significant and what can be ignored in arriving at a decision. A lawyer with good judgment knows when to do nothing and when to do something bold.

These and other statements that represent the spirit of good judgment appear in the course of human history as early as the

137

Old Testament. There one finds a body of writing that biblical scholars label wisdom literature. It includes Ecclesiastes, The Book of Job, Proverbs, and the rulings of King Solomon.

There has been a revival of interest in a wisdom book titled *The Art of Worldly Wisdom* by Baltasar Gracian, a Spanish Jesuit. Gracian's book, written in the sixteenth century, instructs on how to get along in the world by manipulating human nature.

What is best is an apprenticeship with one whose judgment has been tested and proven over an extended period. The apprentice observes the master's instinct in action. The apprentice mimics what is seen and eventually learns the art.

I use the word *instinct*. Instinct is what comes without a need to learn. Birds have good judgment in nest building. But in fact it is not judgment at work. It is the automatic pilot of instinct. With no apprenticeship, the bird chooses the right twigs and knows how to carry the twigs to a well-selected tree. The bird knows the carpentry required to construct a nest that defies the cruel north wind.

Although most of mankind's instincts are ill-defined, there is one that we are all aware of, the instinct for self-preservation. It directs us to find ways to survive, no matter the peril. It overrides both intelligence and learned behavior. It is stronger in some than in others. It may be that in those where it is especially strong it appears as good judgment in dealing with a close call.

Good judgment may consist in knowing when specialized knowledge is required. However instinct may be the decisive element between adversaries who both have specialized knowledge. The chess game analogy comes to mind.

Those with good judgment do not hold it in fee simple. It is good judgment to know when the magic has departed and gone to others.

We are so put together that our bodies contain elements specifically designed to suppress good judgment. It was bad judgment for the king of England to abandon his throne for a Baltimore woman who, judging by most accounts, was a self-seeking materialistic second-rater. King Edward had the best advice of those with proven good judgment. But the king, who was to become a duke, was unable to accept good advice. Why? Well, Arthur Schopenhauer tells us why:

> Next to the love of life, it [sexual love] shows itself here as the strongest and most active of all motives, and incessantly lays claim to half the powers and thoughts of the younger portion of mankind. It is the ultimate goal of almost all human effort; it has an unfavourable influence on the most important affairs, interrupts every hour the most serious occupations, and sometimes perplexes for a while even the greatest minds. It does not hesitate to intrude with its trash, and to interfere with the negotiations of statesmen and the investigations of the learned. It knows how to slip its love-notes and ringlets even into ministerial portfolios and philosophical manuscripts. Every day it brews and hatches the worst and most perplexing quarrels and disputes, destroys the most valuable relationships, and breaks the strongest bonds. It demands the sacrifice some times of life or health, sometimes of wealth, position, and happiness. Indeed, it robs of all conscience those who were previously honourable and upright, and makes traitors of those who have hitherto been loyal and faithful. Accordingly, it appears on the whole as a malevolent demon, striving to pervert, to confuse, and to overthrow everything.

This does not necessarily mean that the Duke of Windsor could not give good advice to others. Lawyers whose personal lives are chaotic get big fees for giving good advice to others.

The lawyers I meet whose judgment is especially good avoid predicating a decision on subjective elements such as judicial idiosyncrasy and convoluted theories of human motivation. Those with good judgment fasten on to what is objective—the facts and the law. Add to that a dash of self-doubt, a sense of what is beyond the immediate, and a mature tolerance for the fact that nothing goes as planned and nothing is as good as it looks. They distinguish between a false optimism based on tarot cards and a reading of the documents line-by-line.

INDECISION

Each trade and each profession stamps its practitioner with its characteristic mark. There is a piece of thread on the tailor. There is the glazed eye of the accountant during tax season. The physician has become so accustomed to hero worship by his patients that he treats all about him as his rightful subjects. He is identified by that gentle bending of the body forward, which, in great men, must be supposed to be the effect of an habitual condescending attention to the applications of their inferiors.

What does the practice of law do to the lawyer? What does continued exposure to disputation do to his mind? William Hazlitt's essay, "On Thought and Action," gives this case history:

Abraham Tucker relates of a friend of his, an old special pleader, that once coming out of his chambers in the Temple with him to take a walk, he hesitated at the bottom of the stairs which way to go—proposed different

directions, to Charing Cross, to St. Paul's—found some
objection to them all, and at last turned back for want of
a casting motive to incline the scale. Tucker gives this as
an instance of professional indecision or of that temper of
mind which having been long used to weigh the reasons
for things with scrupulous exactness, could not come
to any conclusion at all on the spur of the occasion, or
without some grave distinction to justify its choice.

I know a busy negligence lawyer who has grappled with the
facts of so many automobile collisions that his mind is now an
intersection of uncertainties, a crossroad of indecision.

The man of action is the soldier. But he also can be reduced
to indecision if, like the lawyer, he is poised between attack and
retreat. General McClellan's indecision so provoked President
Lincoln (a lawyer and hence an expert on indecision) that Lincoln wrote:

My dear McClellan:

If you do not want to use the army I should like
to borrow it for a while.

Even the lawyer who has donned the robe and picked up the
gavel is not shielded from the malady. Here is a bit of testimony
given at a hearing before the Committee on the Judiciary of the
United States Senate on February 15, 1966:

Judge Biggs: We had another case many years ago in
which a judge also had developed what I think was a
form of illness. He was unable to decide cases. He had
a backlog of some one hundred and twenty five unde-
cided cases, and he could not decide them.

You can see by this excerpt that we are not dealing with a trifle. But I would not have brought up the subject unless I could supply a cure for the war 'twixt will and will not. Which is the best? Well, that is another matter and for another time.

KEEPING SECRETS

Whom a statesman trusts at all he should trust largely, not to say unboundedly; and he should avow his trust to the world. In nine cases out of ten of betrayed confidence in affairs of state, vanity is the traitor. When a man comes into possession of some chance secrets now and then—some one or two—he is tempted to parade them to this friend. But when he is known to be trusted with all manner of secrets, his vanity is interested, not to show them, but to show that he can keep them. And his fidelity of heart is also better secured.

Sir Henry Taylor

Sir Henry makes two points. The first point is obvious. It is the vanity of being known to be trusted with a secret that impels me to disclose it. I prove I am someone of importance by disclosing the secret that someone of established importance has entrusted to me.

Sir Henry's second point is not so obvious. He explains how vanity is used to keep a secret. In order to preserve my reputation as one who can keep a secret, I must not give secrets away. Vanity overcomes vanity.

There is a pleasure in remaining silent when others speak with authority concerning things they don't know about and that I do know about because of secret information. It is the pleasure of certainty held in reserve. It is *prana* pleasure. Prana is the vital energy that the yogi masters say rises or falls in accordance with our doing right or doing wrong according to our personal code of honor. The stronger the impulse to tell a secret, the greater the victory in remaining silent and the better the *prana*.

Social beings, as we are, we need secrets. We protect ourselves against our enemies with our secrets. Battle plans are highly secret. In World War II the United States broke the Japanese code and Great Britain broke the German code. Winston Churchill said this secret was so valuable that it must be protected by a bodyguard of lies. Secrecy for some is a full-time occupation.

Lawyers must keep secret what their clients tell them. We are an exclusive group that has access to other people's secrets. We are in the know.

A lawyer with a good secret is a natural target for a journalist. It is the lawyer's obligation to keep the secret, and it is the journalist's obligation to discover the secret. The journalist relies on flattery to get things moving. The journalist puts in a call to the lawyer. He says he values the lawyer's opinion, the lawyer has a fine reputation, the lawyer is thought to be more competent than other lawyers.

When flattery of this type is administered, the lawyer has no desire to conclude the conversation. Good manners require the lawyer to give something in return for this flattery. He hints at what he knows. He speaks without attribution, off the record, don't mention me, I will deny it. As the lawyer continues to talk, he hears the clicking of the journalist's computer keyboard.

There is an assumption that skill in keeping secrets comes with the reading of the Rules of Professional Conduct and the cases concerning the attorney-client privilege. Not necessarily so. There are those who are good at keeping client secrets, and there are those who are not so good.

Let me describe a lawyer who was good at keeping secrets. I first met him when he was winding down a long, active career. He had access to the secrets of many people. As you might expect, he was a good listener. He did not hint that he knew more than he was permitted to say. He did not assert opinions based on secret knowledge. He told no anecdotes involving his connections with well-known people. His conversation invited what others knew rather than what he knew.

The attorney-client privilege commenced long ago in England. It was the barrister's personal honor that was at issue. He would be dishonored if he revealed anything the client told him. Even the client could not order him to reveal what was said. Over time the English judges narrowed the privilege and changed it around to protect the client and not the honor of the lawyer.

In its present form the privilege is sterile. It gives protection only if the client seeks legal advice. People in real trouble need more than strictly legal advice. They need someone to hear them out, in private, with the comfort that what is said will never be revealed. The religious privilege gives this. The attorney-client privilege should have the same breadth.

Both privileges require that the parties intend that what is said is to be secret. Both require the secrecy to be absolute. The difference is that the religious privilege provides a protected setting of compassion that an experienced lawyer is well suited to administer.

The alternative to what I propose would be for lawyers to add a doctorate in divinity to their doctorate in law. I knew an active local trial lawyer who had both qualifications, theological and legal. She was a minister as well as a lawyer. She did not worry about the technicalities of the attorney-client privilege. She gave ministering solace as needed. What was not covered by the attorney-client privilege was picked up by the religious privilege. The many who unburdened themselves to her were assured that nothing that was said would be revealed. No time. Not ever. Absolutely never.

MONEY

My friends, money is not all. It is not money that will mend
a broken heart or reassemble the fragments of a dream.
Money cannot brighten the hearth nor repair the portals of
a shattered home. I refer, of course, to Confederate money.
                        Attributed to a certain Judge Kelly of Chicago

There is before me a book simply
titled *The Oxford Book of Money*, published by Oxford University
Press. The editor, Kevin Jackson, says *in limine* that the book does
not tell how to make money. What it does is give examples of the
way poets, novelists, dramatists, and wits write about money.

As I read over the selections it becomes clear that money
is so basic to human existence that one could say it is an inborn
characteristic, as language is. The expression that "money talks"
says more than one might think. The inherent human capacity
that supplies an instinct for arithmetical counting must be located
in the same part of the brain where the money chip resides, ready
for action. And what about greed? Is the feel for money invariably

accompanied by some quotient of greed? And does greed carry a quotient of gullibility? Is that why people invest in stock despite an offering memorandum that declares in bold letters that by any rational method of evaluation the stock is worthless? Is that why I receive three telephone calls a week from stock salesmen I have never met? Do they keep calling because somewhere there is documentary evidence that I was gullible once before, and therefore I may be gullible again?

In a quick look through the book I see no writings by lawyers. This is odd. The practice of law is all about money. The client wants the lawyer to help him get money or help him keep the money he has. The papers a lawyer drafts deal with money. Even domestic relations litigation ends up with who gets the money.

In the litigation the first pleading filed is a complaint ending with the *ad damnum* clause demanding money. The responsive pleading, the answer, is a denial that money is owed.

Years ago lawyers did not expect to make large sums of money. The hope was that the income from the law practice would provide enough to make investments in real estate that would provide an income when the law practice expired. This is no longer the case. The young lawyer enters the profession with a burden of college and law school debt. He must make money. He would like to do public interest law, but he must "go corporate" for at least five years to make some money.

The current writing concerning the legal profession deplores the fact that lawyers are in it for the money. Of course lawyers are in it for the money. They should be. Unless a lawyer makes money he will not be a lawyer very long. The real issue is how the lawyer goes about making the money. If he goes about it as Abraham Lincoln did, there will be no complaints. He gave value. But even

Honest Abe had collection problems. Here is his comment concerning a slow-paying client in a letter written in 1842:

> Whatever fees we [Logan and I] earn at a distance, if not paid before, we have noticed we never hear of after the work is done. We, therefore, are growing a little sensitive on that point.

The client who gives the lawyer cash brings good news and bad news. Cash is wonderful. It is immediate. Every lawyer at least once in his career should have the thrill of having a client count out some big bucks right there on the lawyer's desk. But cash carries with it many problems. Where did the client get the cash? Is it stolen money? Is it drug money? There are bank reporting laws concerning cash. It is a violation of the law to make multiple cash bank deposits in order to avoid the reporting requirements. One of these days there will be a law requiring a lawyer to report every cash fee, no matter its size.

Money, standing alone, is innocent. It is fungible and also chameleon. It takes its character from the person who happens to have it. Money in the hands of a generous person represents good money to be used to help somebody who needs money. Money in the hands of someone who wishes to bribe a public official is bad money.

The book *Money* includes Samuel Johnson's comment to Boswell that there are few ways in which a man can be more innocently employed than in getting money. And there is no more innocent enjoyment for a lawyer than spotting a check in among the morning mail's collection of law book advertisements, solicitations for funds, and the usual supply of bills. That is the way to start the day. The check actually was in the mail.

OFFICE AWAY FROM THE OFFICE

One last thought—I have found over the years that it is impossible to do any real thinking and planning and dictating in the office; and it is almost imperative to maintain an office away from your office, either in your home or in some separate location downtown, to which you can go regularly to work without constant interruption.

George L. Mitchell, writing in *The Canadian Bar Journal*

Concentration gathers force from stage to stage only if there are no interruptions. Do you see the way I have put that? Without interruption. That is the key. But interruption is inherent in a law office. There is the telephone, the fax, the email, the cell phone. There are the sights and sounds of the office, each carrying a flash of panic over something undone that must be done.

We do need the office away from the office. A place to plan both the attack and the defense.

Through the generosity of a friend, I once had an office away from the office. I had only a desk and a rocking chair. The silence and the isolation were so different from my office that it took time to get used to it. For the first hour my mind chased around. There was no focus. Gradually I calmed down. I was ready to do one thing at a time. In that blessed state of mind, sitting in the rocking chair, I saw all there was to be seen and much more. I was Sherlock Holmes. I examined not only the writing in the documents, but the quality of the paper it was written on. I correlated dates and events. Connections between facts sprung to mind. Coincidences were charted and evaluated. The area of uncertainty was localized and resolved. What a pleasure it was to work at such a pitch.

Such occasions are rare in a busy practice. The days that can be devoted to one task are so few and far between that we recall them as unusual events.

The only thing worse than being too busy is to be stranded in the practice with too little to do. There seems to be no in-between. The best arrangement is to stay busy and maintain a silent area away from the office. When it all crowds in, retreat into the silence. Read one page at a time. And above all, don't answer the telephone. Let it ring. There—it finally stopped. Who was it? Could it be the big case that would once and for all enhance your career and place you within the charmed circle of great advocates? As a matter of fact, it was the woman who wants to sue the owner of the clock that had the wrong time that caused her to miss her appointment for the new job as interior decorator in residence at the condominium to be built if the loan goes through.

TABLE TALK AND
MATURITY

Talk, talk, talk,
Of peace and war, health, sickness, death, and life,
Of loss and gain, of famine and of store ...
Of turns of fortune, changes in the state,
The falls of fav'rites, projects of the great,
Of old mismanagements, taxations new:
All neither wholly false, nor wholly true.
            Alexander Pope, "The Temple of Fame"

Lawyer talk occurs at odd times and places. It takes place in courthouse corridors. It takes place while waiting for the jury to return its verdict. It takes place at chance meetings on the street. It takes place in airports, at Union Station, and at funerals.

At lunch, the table talk is of law firm breakups, politics, judges, obituaries, whatever happened to what's-his-name, and did you see who just walked in. The talk inevitably turns to a discussion of the current front-page perjury trial. Will the defendant take the stand in his own defense? If he does, the prosecutor will cross-examine the defendant on matters that otherwise would be inadmissible. If he doesn't testify and there is a guilty verdict, he will insist to his lawyer and everyone else that he would have been a great witness and would have acquitted himself. Experienced criminal lawyers put on the record, outside the presence of the jury, the defendant's own statement that he chooses not to testify.

If the defendant insists on testifying, he must avoid the words never and *absolutely*. Life does not deal in absolutes, especially when one is testifying under oath. To say something never happened is a challenge the prosecutor absolutely and enthusiastically accepts.

In English trials, judges and prosecutors are permitted to draw an unfavorable inference when the defendant does not go into the box. Our rules forbid this.

The talk then turns to what the government must prove to get a perjury conviction. One of the senior lawyers at the table takes charge. He opens by saying that unless you have tried and lost a perjury case, you have never been in the big time. He uses words such as *materiality* and *criminal intent*. He lets it be known that his favorite case is *Bronston* v. *United States*. He casually tosses off from memory the citation—409 U.S. 352—and launches into a set speech about the case in which the Supreme Court reversed Bronston's conviction. Bronston's answer under oath was in fact true but intentionally misleading, and a defendant cannot be convicted of perjury when what he said was actually true.

He concludes his much-too-long story by saying President Clinton relied on Bronston when he famously declared, "It depends on what the meaning of the word 'is' is."

What if there is a young lawyer present at the table, a lawyer consumed by ambition, a lawyer who recently had read a law review article about perjury trials? He is anxious to enter the discussion and correct the speaker on the way the courts have been interpreting Bronston by narrowing its application. Should he speak up? He should not, for at least two good reasons.

First, Mr. Know-It-All would be offended. He will never refer a client to this upstart.

Second, the man sitting to his left gives signs of remaining ostentatiously reticent. That is his style. He always chooses to speak last. He will demonstrate that each of the previous speakers missed the key point.

Max Beerbohm, in an essay quoting from James Boswell's The Life of Samuel Johnson, tells us what happened on the afternoon of April 7, 1778, to an unnamed clergyman who did speak and had the audacity to challenge Samuel Johnson. Beerbohm quotes Boswell:

> Boswell: What I want to know is, what sermons afford
> the best specimen of English pulpit eloquence.
> Johnson: We have no sermons addressed to the passions,
> that are good for anything; if you mean that kind of
> eloquence.
> A Clergyman, (unnamed): Were not Dodd's sermons
> addressed to the passions?
> Johnson (redressing the clergyman): They were nothing,
> Sir, be they addressed to what they may.

Then, Beerbohm closes the ring:

> The suddenness of it! Bang!—and the rabbit that had
> popped from its burrow was no more.

Fragmentary, pale, momentary; almost nothing; glimpsed and gone; as it were, a faint human hand thrust up, never to reappear, from beneath the roiling waters of Time, ... Nothing is told of him but that once, abruptly, he asked a question, and received an answer.

There happens to be a woman present at this luncheon. She is a woman with a distinguished legal career. She is privy to client secrets that The Associated Press would like to have. She is thinking to herself that if she were younger she would drop a few hints here and there to show she is the person that people in trouble must consult. But now she has reached the age where all her ambitions have been fulfilled. She has seen good times and bad times. She enjoys sitting back and watching others perform— the know-it-alls. If there is such a thing as Legal Nirvana, free of hatred and delusion, she has reached it. She enjoys the warm contentment of remaining quiet. She is mature.

THE BALLOON NOTE

A lethal commercial instrument. It was a promissory note with monthly interest-only payments all the way down to the final payment, but oh that final payment. It is the big balloon representing the entire unpaid balance. The device was used to sell cars to people who could not afford them. The purchaser was sold, along with the car, tie-in credit life insurance and tie-in collision coverage. There was also a version called the slow balloon. It was a demand note in which the interest is put so high and the monthly payments put so low that the balloon expands with each monthly payment—up, up a little bit higher. An expert in the field describes it as a negative amortizing note.

When the balloon fell due and the victim could not pay, his car was picked up by the repossessor.

Once the car was "repopped" the dealer arranged a friendly sale to create a large spread between the unpaid balance on the note and the friendly sales price. The noteholder then sued the victim for the deficiency.

There is a maxim among arms merchants that every weapon of attack develops its own weapon of defense. In time resourceful lawyers for the victims developed the glove compartment defense. It worked this way: The victim, so it seemed, kept expensive jewelry and priceless family heirlooms in the glove compartment of the car. What happened to these treasures when the ear was repopped? The noteholder wasn't entitled to them, and his having taken possession of the car was chargeable with returning the valuables or paying for the loss. Juries award substantial damages for such losses. Who wants to defend a jury case when your key witness repopped a wage earner's car? The glove compartment defense and/or counterclaim neutralized many deficiency suits. The repossession laws now have been changed to offer some protection to the victim.

Another artifact of times gone by is the confessed judgment note giving the note-holder the right to obtain judgment, *ex parte*, in a summary proceeding, with no defenses allowed. The language in the note authorized the lender to do everything but kidnap the borrower and hold him for ransom.

In the 1950s, Chrysler, Ford, and General Motors each had its captive finance company. As the balloon noteholder, it declared the default, ordered the repossession, and brought the deficiency claim. General Motors Acceptance Corporation brought a deficiency case in which I represented the victim. I filed a counterclaim that gave the appearance of some merit. The trial judge tried to settle the case. He told GMAC's lawyer that he should dismiss GMAC's case and pay some money to get rid of the counterclaim. GMAC's lawyer agreed with the suggestion, but he said he could not act on it. When asked why, he said, "Look at who the plaintiff is. It is the General Motors

Acceptance Corporation. Under its corporate charter it can only
accept money. It is not authorized to disburse money. Before I
could pay any money out I would have to change the corporate
charter, and I cannot recommend that to General Motors." Even
as green as I was at the time, I recognized I was in the presence
of a talented negotiator.

A GOOD METAPHOR

There are anecdotes, metaphors, and maxims that clinch the facts and the law under discussion. One of these clinchers I heard was used by John Wilson.

Wilson had a remarkable career. With only a few partners he represented local banks, department stores, insurance companies, utilities, and builders.

No one enjoyed the law practice more than Wilson did. His office law library and his home law library were where he wanted to be when he was not in court.

When addressing the court, he placed on the rostrum the books he was to use, piling the books, one on top of the other. After reading the relevant passage from the book on top, he carelessly tossed it aside and went to the next one. When he completed his presentation, he gathered up the books in both arms and lovingly carried them back to counsel's table.

I had an occasion to be in Wilson's office when a lawyer we both knew was discussing a personal problem. The lawyer, after going over the facts, said, "John, there it is, and I think if I don't do anything, it will, like many things, just go away. What do you think?" Wilson thought for a minute and said, "Frank, I think you are sitting on a crack that is expanding. It won't go away." A crack that is expanding. A perceptive insight.

In complicated and unsettled situations, Wilson followed the maxim that it is best to let someone else make the first move. He judged things on the recoil.

I learned a helpful story from William Gardner. He, too, had a fine legal mind, tempered by sympathy for the underdog. Bill had seen life from many angles, and he knew how difficult it could be for most people. I heard him repeat the words "Be kind. Everyone you meet is fighting a great battle." As a judge he did not lecture the people who were before him. He ruled with no personal comments directed at the losing party. He remained neutral.

I was in a case with Bill in which our client wanted to litigate a matter of no particular importance for the sole purpose of getting even with someone. I tried to explain to the client that bringing the case would be a mistake. It would be costly and the defendant would find some way to bring a nasty counterclaim. I was getting nowhere. The client turned to Bill and said, "Bill, what do you think?" Bill said, "Let me tell you a story my father told me. A man was standing right near a cesspool. He was probing it with a stick. His friend said to him, 'Why are you standing so close to the edge of that bad-smelling cesspool?' The man said, 'Ordinarily, I would not go near a cesspool, but I dropped my lunch in there and I am trying to get it out.'"

Alcohol has been a problem for lawyers, perhaps more so in the past than now. I have worked with lawyers who were recovering alcoholics. Without exception these men and one woman had a grade-A sense of humor, and they hesitated to criticize those who may have departed from what we like to believe is the path of virtue.

This brings me to a lawyer I will call Leo Cooke. I don't know if his ability to concentrate fully on the representation of a client and at the same time remain detached was brought about by his long but finally successful struggle with alcohol. He had an interest in English literature. In one of our long (but non-alcoholic) conversations I asked him how it was that he could be so involved and remain detached. He referred me to a passage in Leonard Woolf's autobiography:

> I was born an introspective intellectual, and the man or woman who is by nature addicted to introspection gets into the habit, after the age of 15 or 16, of feeling himself often intensely as "I" and yet at the same time of seeing himself out of the corner of his eye as a "not I," a stranger acting a part upon a stage. I always feel, from moment to moment, that my life and the life around me is immediately and extraordinarily real, concrete, and yet at the same time there is something absurdly unreal about it, because, knowing too well what I am really like inside, I cannot avoid continually watching myself playing a part upon a stage.

Lawyers play two roles. There is the "I" that makes the mistakes. There is the "not I," the stoic who stands back and watches.

ODDS & ENDS

The Briefless Barrister
A Ballad

An Attorney was taking a turn,
  In shabby habiliments drest;
His coat it was shockingly worn,
  And the rust had invested his vest.

His breeches had suffered a breach,
  His linen and worsted were worse;
He had scarce a whole crown in his hat,
  And not half a crown in his purse.

And thus as he wandered along,
  A cheerless and comfortless elf,
He sought for relief in a song,
  Or complainingly talked to himself: —

"Unfortunate man that I am!
  I've never a client but grief:
The case is, I've no case at all,
  And in brief, I've ne'er had a brief!

"I've waited and waited in vain,
  Expecting an 'opening' to find,
Where an honest young lawyer might gain
  Some reward for toil of his mind.

"'Tis not that I'm wanting in law,
  Or lack an intelligent face,

169

That others have cases to plead,
    While I have to plead for a case.

"Oh, how can a modest young man
    E'er hope for the smallest progression,—
The profession's already so full
    Of lawyers so full of profession!"

While thus he was strolling around
    His eye accidentally fell
On a very deep hole in the ground,
    And he sighed to himself, "It is well!"

To curb his emotions, he sat
    On the curbstone the space of a minute,
Then cried, "Here's an opening at last!"
    And in less than a jiffy was in it!

Next morning twelve citizens came
    ('Twas the coroner bade them attend),
To the end it might be determined
    How the man had determined his end!

"The man was a lawyer, I hear,"
    Quoth the foreman, who sat on the corse.
"A lawyer? Alas!" said another,
    "Undoubtedly died of remorse!"

A third said, "He knew the deceased,
    An attorney well versed in the laws,

And as to the cause of his death,
    'Twas no doubt for the want of a cause."

The jury decided at length,
    After solemnly weighing the matter,
That the lawyer was drownded, because
    He could not keep his head above water!

John Godfrey Saxe

CONVERGING ON A DIVERGENCE

There is dissatisfaction with the adversary system of justice. It is too adversarial. It is too costly. It may turn on itself and produce injustice rather than justice. It lost its way between Federal Rules 26 through 37, the civil discovery rules. In an effort to do away with surprise it suffocated itself. Despite the criticism, its proponents give powerful arguments to justify its continuation. They contend that in most cases it remains the best way to get at the truth.

The core of the controversy turns on whether counsel's devotion to client interests interferes too often with service to the higher principles of justice even if such service requires deserting the client.

E. F. Schumacher, in his *A Guide for the Perplexed*, tells us that unsolved problems create anguish for those with orderly minds, such as lawyers. We like to deal with ideas that bring certainty beyond a reasonable doubt. Schumacher says all problems divide themselves into two categories: convergent problems and divergent problems.

To illustrate a convergent problem, Schumacher uses the quest for the best design of a two-wheeled bicycle. As each proponent offers solutions, each finds that the solutions gradually converge and the best design emerges. Why is this so? It is because the best design is determined by laws of engineering and inanimate nature. Measurements and tests give an immediate correction if the design is wrong. The more we study a convergent problem, the better the solution.

Legal disputes present a divergent problem. Experts during a trial contradict each other. The more abstract the opinions, the more disagreement. History is filled with wars for which thousands died and now no one can tell just what the fight was about or why it lasted so long. Things that cannot be proved are the things that trigger the strongest emotions.

Schumacher says that when we are dealing with a divergent problem, we can deal with it only if we get above it. We must abandon any effort at a yes or no, right or wrong answer.

E=PROCRASTINATION= MC^2

This day and age we're living in gives cause for apprehension, with speed and new inventions and things like the third dimension. Yet we get a trifle weary of Mr. Einstein's theory, so we must get down to earth at times, relieve the tension.

Do these words sound familiar? They are the words to the song "As Time Goes By" ("You must remember this / A kiss is still a kiss"). This wistful 1930's tune was revived in the 1940's movie *Casablanca* with Bogie and Ingrid.

The national public television produced a show on Albert Einstein's 100th anniversary of $E=mc^2$. I had hoped that, once and for all, I would get an understandable explanation of $E=mc^2$. I knew that E means energy and that m means mass and that c means the speed of light. Beyond that I knew nothing more.

Within the first hour of watching the program I became uneasy. There were the details of Einstein's private life, a life with the same contradictions and mistakes that we all have, but no understandable explanation of $E=mc^2$. I also heard repeated in a defiant way that nothing can be faster than the speed of light, but nobody explained why. So I got a little weary of Mr. Einstein's theory, and I switched channels to the White Sox-Angels playoffs.

The next day I spoke with a physicist friend and asked if he watched the program. He said he watched for a half-hour, and when Einstein did not get a base hit he turned back to the White Sox. I was not to be put off. I asked him why it is that nothing can be faster than light.

Here is his explanation, which I pass on to you. Assume I have a speed machine that can, in fact, go faster than the speed of light. I get on board and speed back along the light beam that is coming toward me. I go so fast that I go back faster than light. I go so fast I overtake the events of the past. I see myself in H. D. Cooke Grammar School. There are now two of us, the grown man and the callow youth, both together at the same time. Of course this cannot be done, except in the movies.

I next asked my friend, what is energy? He said energy is movement. Everything in the universe is moving. The earth is spinning and moving around the sun, which is moving around all the other constellations. Stillness is an illusion. Nothing stands still. I asked how he connects this up with the so-called general theory. He then took a call on his cell phone.

For a moment I thought I had it. Time and space, and mass and light, and the movement of light and energy, and the atomic bomb that explodes with the speed of light squared, and therefore … but I lose the thread.

I took a look at Max Beerbohm's essay, "A Note on the Einstein Theory." The incomparable Max included in his essay an account by a friend of Einstein's. This friend said Einstein was a very human person. He liked to play the fiddle. He liked to smoke a pipe and daydream. He was not a man in a hurry about things. Folded into the pages of Beerbohm's essay was a faded newspaper clipping reporting that Albert Einstein liked to put things off. He was a procrastinator.

Once I read that, I felt I knew the man. Was the discovery of $E=mc^2$ Einstein's way of avoiding the things he should have done? That would be an interesting discovery. I would have liked to cross-examine him on that point. He might be a genius in quantum physics, time, light, and gravity, but no match for me concerning procrastination. I would force him to concede that anyone can do any amount of work provided it's not work he is supposed to do. I learned the art of procrastination in the best school there is—practicing law. There is no better place. Lawyers do it. Judges do it. Even law professors up at Yale do it.

The best lawyers I have known are the best at contriving ways to delay making a decision. What's the rush?

One of the causes of procrastination is the deadline. There are hundreds of deadlines hidden in the Federal Rules of Civil Procedure, the Federal Rules of Evidence, the local rules, the chambers rules, the appellate rules, the administrative rules, and the annotations to the rules. The fact that something must be done by a specified date does get things done, but it often works against getting things done. The point was made by Leonard Woolf describing his friend Desmond McCarthy:

> [He] told me then that he really suffered from a disease:
> the moment he knew that he ought to do some thing,
> no matter what that some thing was, he felt absolutely
> unable to do it and would do anything else in order to

prevent himself from doing it. It did not matter what "it" might be; it might be something which he actually wanted to do, but if it was also something which he knew he ought to do, he would find himself doing something which he did not want to do in order to prevent himself doing something which he ought to do and wanted to do.

We delay things, hoping they will work themselves out. What a pleasure it is to have your adversary call and ask you to consent to a continuance, a continuance you desperately needed. Delay cools tempers and opens up additional reasons for delay.

Let me close with some advice. When you realize you are getting caught in a procrastination mental block, you must immediately turn the assignment over to someone else. The person you give the assignment to will do it right away. He has his own mental blocks, and he will welcome an assignment that distracts him from what he should be doing, which for some reason he cannot do. Give me a call and we will work a trade.

FIGHTING THE BLUES
WITH THE FINE ARTS

To go to court is to court disappointment. A lawyer who never lost a case has tried few cases. There are disappointments even when the case isn't tried. There is motions court—the long and the short. If going to court is part of your practice, you must find a way to fight the blues that accompany the inevitable disappointments inherent in the adversary system. If your practice is right here in Washington, you are in luck. Both the local and the federal courts are located between two retreats where one can restore equilibrium. They are the National Gallery of Art and the National Portrait Gallery.

The National Gallery of Art is just south of the United States District Court. If you have just been dealt an adverse ruling by a judge who does not understand summary judgment, I suggest when you leave the courthouse you stroll down to the National Gallery and refresh yourself surrounded by priceless works of art.

Enter the main building, walk up to the second floor and turn left and wander around among the Impressionists. There is something a lawyer can learn from Monet's and Pissarro's Paris street scenes. Up close they are an incomprehensible clutter of colored dots and dashes. Stand back a few feet and they become a clearly recognizable busy Parisian street. One might say that hundreds of facts, relevant and not so relevant, are converted by the artist into a winning picture that one takes in at a glance. The art of the advocate.

Subtlety is also part of the advocate's art. Things are never black and white. It is the shades of gray that make the difference. Take a look at Manet's Death of a Toreador. Manet sparingly used the blacks and whites to outline the body of the toreador and a dot of red to show the toreador's bleeding wound. In between are the 20 shades of gray that show the skill of the artist.

If the case you lose was tried in the local Superior Court you leave the court and walk north to 8th and F Streets. There you find the National Portrait Gallery. Within it is inspiration. You will see a stirring portrait of Theodore R. Roosevelt, caught by the artist in the act of reciting these stirring words:

Far better it is to dare mighty things, to win glorious triumphs, even though checkered by failure, than to take rank with those poor spirits who neither enjoy much nor suffer much, because they live in the gray twilight that knows not victory nor defeat.

Both the National Portrait Gallery and the National Gallery of Art have interior courtyards where one sits alone and meditates and considers life's big questions, such as, Why didn't I take another deposition? Why did I assume that the judge had read the papers?

Winston Churchill, in his book *Painting as a Pastime*, says there are many remedies for life's disappointments. He identifies exercise, travel, play, and other diversions. He then says that what is common to all these things is the need to change course when things go bad. He discovered that the best change for him was painting. "Happy are the painters, for they shall not be lonely. Light and color, peace and hope, will keep them company to the end, or almost to the end, of the day." When Churchill was in his state of depression during the lonely 1930's, an artist friend told him to buy a paint box, paints, and some big brushes. Churchill was told that the quality that was needed to get started was not years devoted to the study of drawing, perspective, and the science of color. He was too old for that. All he needed was what he had, courage and audacity. Get big splashes of paint on a canvas, and the sooner the better. He discovered that big brushes and lots of paint bring good luck to a canvas. He discovered what everyone who paints discovers. Within the smears themselves one sees well drawn landscapes and portraits.

Churchill's studio is preserved at Chartwell, his estate outside London. It is worth a trip to Chartwell just to see Churchill's painting arrangements. The studio is in a little house away from the main house. Visitors are told it is maintained just as it was when Churchill used it. As one can see, he used big brushes and lots of paint. Churchill had advantages that most amateurs do not have. He had skilled painters as friends and when he encountered a problem beyond his competence, he had an artist friend look over his shoulder and give him some advice.

There is a picture in the Chartwell main house of Churchill at lunch with his professional artist friends. One of the artists in the photograph is Walter Sickert, whose influence can be detected in Churchill's landscapes. Sickert liked to paint the interiors of music halls and the second-rate music hall performers.

A few years ago I came across a book of Sickert's paintings. It looked to me, in my own spirit of audacity, that Sickert's painting called *That Wonderful Mother of Mine* would be easy to copy. It is a picture of a music hall singer all dressed up in battered white tie and tails, standing at the footlights singing a sentimental ballad in memory of his wonderful mother. Audacity carried me forward, and the picture turned out to be worth my investing in a moderately expensive frame.

The effort to copy the painting of a skilled artist, just the making of the effort, teaches more about the art and the appreciation of painting than hours of abstract lectures. I commend it to you. It makes no difference that you have no talent. In fact the absence of talent gives you an insight into the complicated sleight of hand required of the professional artist. Better off doing some work with the oils and brushes than standing in line for a Van Gogh exhibit.

I BELIEVE IT

Yes, I believe everything; you cannot tell me anything that
I cannot believe. That the forbidden fruit of Paradise was
an apple presents no difficulties to me; nor that mermaids
sing when combing their hair and swans when dying, that
ostriches eat keys and a whale ate Jonah, that a remora can
stay a ship, and the cockatrice, who is hatched by a road out
of the egg of a cock, slay a man by a glance.

Rebecca West

Of course the renowned
journalist and author Rebecca West did not believe a word of it.
She said it with a wink of an eye. Her comment is ironic. Samuel
Johnson defined irony as "a mode of speech of which the meaning is contrary to the words."

H. L. Mencken, the Baltimore sage, had the gift of irony.
He did not like judges (and, on occasion, judges did not like
him), and he had his fun with them. In his reminiscence titled
Heathen Days, he recalls prohibition in New York City:

That was in the primitive days when New York still
bristled with peepholes and it was impossible to get
into a strange place without a letter from a judge ...

Come to think of it, the practice of law is ironic. As lawyers
we are prepared to believe everything, just like Rebecca West.
We are in the believing line of business. Where nothing is certain
(the Supreme Court's 5–4 opinions with 3 concurring), we use
the plausible.

A prospective client tells us an unbelievable story. We run it
through the conflicts check. If there is no conflict and the client
is what is known as well-fixed, we are inclined to believe it.

We believe someone who says he is entitled to a $100
million separation bonus for running a public company into
bankruptcy.

We believe someone with no assets and no job can make
monthly mortgage payments of $5,000.

We believe someone with no assets and no job should be
given a credit card.

We believe people who seek political power are solely interested in doing so for the public good.

We believe the Wall Street brokerage house that claims in
its splashy television ads that it will wisely invest your money,
while at the same time *The Wall Street Journal* reports its loss of
$3.2 billion in subprime loans held for its own account.

We believe the three-man compensation committee always
deals fairly in distributing the year-end bonuses.

We believe the evidentiary rules, which declare that a dying
declaration or an excited utterance is the truth, the whole truth,
and nothing but the truth.

We believe a person who passes the bar exam is qualified to give advice on tax law, limited liability partnership agreements, international mediation, and atomic energy regulations.

We believe someone who is to be electrocuted and is suffering from a mental illness must be treated and rehabilitated so he can qualify to be legally executed.

We believe juries are always right when we win and wrong when we lose.

I knew a lawyer who believed nothing. His days were filled with suspicion. He earned his law degree by going to night school and working as an investigator for a life insurance company during the day. He had the persistence and the tenacity of Barton Keyes, the character Edward G. Robinson plays in the 1944 version of *Double Indemnity.*

This lawyer I am describing felt inferior to those with better credentials. He should not have. In the trial practice, a good investigator is worth three lawyers. As far as I knew, his conduct was ethical, perhaps more so than those who condescended to him.

He was not cunning by nature, but he felt that the cunning of others required him to resort to being as cunning as his opponents.

I also knew a lawyer who believed just about everything. I once asked him if his trust in others had been betrayed. He said he could recall only a few occasions.

Piero Calamandrei, one of Italy's leading authorities on civil procedure, wrote this interesting musing in *Eulogy of Judges*:

> If a lawyer enters the courtroom armed with subter-
> fuge and clever dialectics, if he relies upon the partiality
> of the judges or their corruptibility instead of relying

upon honest argument, he should not be surprised to find himself not in an austere temple of justice but rather in a hall of mirrors like those one finds at fairs, where from every wall his intrigues return to him multiplied and distorted. To find purity in the courtroom, one must enter with a pure heart. Even here what Father Christopher said applies: *"Omnia munda mundis"* "Things are pure to the pure in heart".

Looking back over the years, I recall only two times I was deliberately lied to. On one of those occasions, the lawyer in question and I were co-counsel in a personal injury case, representing the plaintiffs. We agreed to work together and not negotiate separately with the defendant's insurance counsel.

One day co-counsel came to me and said he had settled his case without telling me—a clear breach of our agreement. However, he said, the counsel for the insurance company would not pay the agreed upon settlement. He wanted to warn me that I should never accept the word of those bad insurance people.

KAFKAESQUE

Franz Kafka's name, converted into the adjective *Kafkaesque*, proves to me useful in describing the indescribable.

Its use by the Supreme Court of the United States makes the point:

> The proposed plant [atomic energy plant] underwent an incredibly extensive review. The report filed and reviewed literally fills books. The proceedings took years, and the actual hearings themselves over two weeks. To then nullify that effort seven years later because one report refers to other problems, which problems admittedly have been discussed at length in other reports available to the public, borders on the Kafkaesque.
>
> *Vermont Yankee Nuclear Power Corp.* v.
> *Natural Resources Defense Council Inc.*,
> 98 S. Ct. 1197, 435 U.S. 519 (1978)

Kafkaesque is the enforcement of rules of procedure to the point of irrationality. It is the conversion of the simple into the complex. It is the inexorable bureaucratic legal process grinding the helpless individual. It is the irrational combined with staying power. It is the nightmare become real. It is the anonymous voice that interrupts your telephone call and says, "If you want to make a telephone call, please hang up and ..." It is the impossibility of filing a motion in a court encrusted by local rules. It is the arrogance of clerks. It is a prosecutor with an unlimited budget.

It includes heroic efforts to save the life of a man sentenced to death so he can be electrocuted in good health. It includes all Rule 11 proceedings. It is a refusal by the court to accept a misdemeanor plea because the defendant is incompetent and then the court's ordering the indeterminate commitment of the defendant to a mental institution until he can prove he is competent.

It is statutes, rules, codes, and regulations that are a tangle of prolixity.

After law school Franz Kafka (1883–1924) took a job with the Workers Accident Insurance Company for the Kingdom of Bohemia in Prague, Czechoslovakia, Poric Strasse 7. He worked there from 1908 until his retirement in 1922.

Kafka was assigned to the workers' compensation claims department. A workers' compensation claim file contains forms that identify the injured employee, the employee's vital statistics, and the employer's and employee's version of the accident.

There is always a conflict between the employer's version and the injured person's version. Each allegation is the subject of an affidavit covered over with notarized seals and ribbons. Medical reports either corroborate or discredit the worker's claim of injury.

It was Kafka's assignment to review the files and weigh the employee's allegations against those of the employer, and then he must rule. Kafka's files piled up on the floor, on the chairs, on the desks, and on the windowsills. Kafka never had enough information to justify a decision. He needed more medical reports, more witness statements, more affidavits, more memoranda. But he never needed to see and talk to the claimant.

Kafka took in the bureaucratic process as both an outsider and an insider. He was a double agent. He was the person he detested. He knew that until he, acting as the bureaucrat in charge, decided in favor of the injured party, the insurance company retained the funds. Every day's mail brought packets of letters importuning Kafka for the decisive action he was incapable of taking.

Franz Kafka, all his life, wrote stories. In his stories his characters are so poisoned by the bureaucratic secretion that they believe any governmental horror is not only possible but likely.

In Kafka's story The Trial, the first sentence is, "Someone must have been telling lies about Joseph K., for without having done anything wrong he was arrested one fine morning." That sentence, so the critic Malcolm Bradbury declared, is one of the most famous openings in all literature. Its words evoke reality and horror in the proper mixture of the real and the surreal.

Joseph K. knows he is guilty of something. Isn't everybody? Don't prosecutors say that the federal criminal code is so comprehensive that even a denial of guilt is prosecutable as a false statement felony under 18 U.S.C. § 1001?

What Joseph K. wants to know from his prosecutors is just what he did wrong. Despite all the procedural safeguards, he is put to death without getting an answer.

None of Kafka's stories was published during his life-time. Once published after his death, they became a part of the twentieth-century canon. He was, according to Bradbury, "one of the most profoundly troubling, as well as the most modern, of our twentieth-century writers."

OLD FILES

Summertime is the time to throw out old files, folders marked pleadings, correspondence, and memos of law, fact and fiction. The papers I am looking at contain strong language and veiled threats of action to be taken unless. Each was answered in the proper retaliatory tone. The words "for the record" appear here and there.

And here are the files of a client who called every day in hopes that his adversary had been delivered a procedural blow from which Napoleon himself could not recover. Let us hope his litigation mania is in remission and he has turned his focus on something constructive.

Files themselves change over the years. In the 1930's they consisted of long paper pockets in which the court papers were folded and inserted. File cabinets were narrow and accommodating to the arrangement. The law offices of years gone by are seen in etchings showing the haphazard nature of the filing system. The spirit is Dickensian with overtones of *Bartelby, the Scrivener.*

The legal-size requirement has been abandoned by most courts in favor of letter size. *Mellinkoff's Dictionary of American Legal Usage* defines a file as "the bundle of legal papers relating to a case or other official proceeding." The use of the word "bundle" catches the spirit.

Old files, like old newspapers, are drained of all capacity to cause fear. Disturbing when current, they are neutralized by the passage of time, which reveals how things turned out, who won, who lost—and now, who cares?

I read the old pleadings and memoranda in support of this and that to which I was proud to have signed my name. They do not read as well now as when warm with partisan indignation.

I have given up using strong language in pleadings and papers. It is a coin of little value. If I were a judge I would be suspicious of any case that required the support of personal attacks combined with words like "outrageous," "frivolous," or "entirely misleading." Occasionally a personal attack appears in a dissenting opinion of the Supreme Court. What does it accomplish? Why was the dissenter unable to convince the majority through the customary channels of civilized communication?

And none of it shows real imagination. Compare it with Disraeli's description of Gladstone: "A sophisticated rhetorician, inebriated with the exuberance of his own verbosity, and gifted with an egotistical imagination that can at all times command an interminable and inconsistent series of arguments to malign an opponent and glorify himself."

There, my friends, is *ad hominem*.

I have noticed that papers filed by governmental agencies and the Department of Justice use the denunciatory style. It is rare that a representative of the greatest power that ever existed has the magnanimity to concede that a free citizen who pays taxes may have said something of merit. The Pavlovian response is more frequent—the plaintiffs' assertions are entirely without merit.

I shall throw these old files right over my shoulder into a big trash hamper. Burying the dead brings a unique exhilaration. But a question arises: How long must client files be retained? What are the rules? Always rules. To hell with the rules, this trash must go.

RELEVANCE

Irrelevance can be highly enlightening. The witness who starts with what she had for breakfast and remembers it was Thursday because her husband's sister had come down with the measles when she shouldn't have, if she had only gone to the other doctor, the one with glasses—should be a delight to the judge's heart and make the jury feel at home. Behind this leisurely sweep of incident they can follow her as they please, and it will give them at least her barometric pressure at the time when she signed the note at the bank without reading it.

Curtis Bok

I
f a judge were required to conduct a trial using only one rule of evidence, what rule would it be? It must be a rule defining relevance. Without that rule a trial would be interminable. One thing leads to another and there is always something else. An argument can be made that no event can be understood without knowledge of all preceding events extending back to the Book of Genesis.

Justice Oliver Wendell Holmes, when a state court judge, declared that the rule of relevance is the necessary concession to the shortness of life. The Federal Rules of Evidence define relevant evidence as evidence that makes the existence of any fact that is of consequence to the determination of the action more probable or less probable than it would be without the evidence.

Such a definition gives the trial judge a right to treat whatever is offered as relevant. There is the companion rule that gives the judge discretion to exclude evidence, although relevant, when the judge believes that the probative value of the evidence is substantially outweighed by its consumption in time, by its unfair prejudice, or because the evidence may confuse or mislead the jury.

These two rules, the rule of inclusion and the rule of exclusion, invite the judge to find the nice balance that brings in the necessary probative evidence and casts out the unnecessary evidence that takes up more of the court's time than it is worth.

Evidence of marginal value is costly in two ways. First, there is the time it takes to present the evidence. Then there is the time it takes the opponent to offer the explanatory facts. Once the process begins, it may be difficult to stop. Newton's law comes into play: For every action there is an equal but opposite reaction.

The fundamental principles are simple, but the correct application requires an instinct on the part of both the lawyers and the presiding judge. Once the lawyers know that the judge has that instinct, the lawyers move the case ahead. But what happens when the lawyers sense that the judge is insecure?

Here is the state of mind of a lawyer tuning himself up to confuse and mislead the judge as long as the judge allows it.

It is taken from the English play, *The Plain Dealer*, by William
Wycherley, written some 300 years ago—

> I will, as I see cause, extenuate or examplify [sic] matter
> of fact; baffle truth with impudence; answer exceptions
> with questions, though never so impertinent; for reasons
> give 'em words; for law and equity, tropes and figures;
> and so relax and enervate the sinews of their argument
> with the oil of my eloquence. But when my lungs can
> reason no longer, and not be able to say anything more
> for our cause, say everything of our adversary; whose
> reputation, though never so clear and evident in the eye
> of the world, yet with sharp invectives—with poignant
> and sour invectives, I say, I will deface, wipe out, and
> obliterate his fair reputation, even as a record with the
> juice of lemons; and tell such a story, (for the truth on't
> is, all that we can do for our client in chancery, is telling
> a story,) a fine story, a long story, such a story—

In that brief passage is to be found much that goes on today.
The more things change, the more ...

SLEUTH

Ayear's work as a detective on a city police force is an asset for anyone interested in trial work. It is more valuable than A's in Evidence and Civil Procedure. Facts decide most cases. Detectives deal with facts.

A good detective gathers the facts without bias and prejudice. In a trial the judge instructs the jurors to go about their work without bias and prejudice because bias and prejudice distort, deceive, mislead, and often conceal the obvious.

The detective and the lawyer are engaged in what Thomas Huxley (1825–1895) calls retrospective prophecy. Retrospective prophecy deals with the past, the relation between cause and effect, starting with the effect and identifying the cause. Let us say a lawyer is presented a case involving an intersection collision. The lawyer must go backward from the collision. From the effect to cause, effect to cause. Sherlock Holmes (no relation to the justice) said, "All life is a great chain, the nature of which is known whenever we are shown a single link of it."

Sherlock Holmes used what appeared to be insignificant clues to unravel the significant events in the life of a witness. The depth of a footprint discloses that the walker had a left-foot limp. The weave of an abandoned hat tells Holmes that the witness spent time in Ceylon.

Conan Doyle said that the character of Sherlock Holmes was modeled, in large part, on that of Joseph Bell, an Edinburgh surgeon. Bell used a patient's symptoms to get at the person himself. Bell would say to his students, "I am not quite sure whether this man is a cork-cutter or a slater. I observe a slight callus, or hardening, on one side of his fourth finger and a little thickening on the outside of his thumb, and that is a sure sign that he is either one or the other."

Charles Darwin gave us the masterpiece of retrospective prophecy. It was there for all to see, awaiting the person who would examine the facts without bias and prejudice. Darwin did just that. Thomas Huxley said after reading *On the Origin of Species*, "How stupid not to have thought of that."

Once the lawyer establishes the remote cause and its connection to the events that make up the case, the lawyer looks for the law that puts the blame on his adversary. This is the easy part of the case. The law rests safely in the books. It is always at home. It never ducks a subpoena. It does not have a faulty memory.

My own career as a detective commenced when I worked for the Willmark Detective Agency. My friend Harry Lacy and I were hired by Willmark in 1945. If Willmark had a competent human resources officer, he would never have hired us. It would have been apparent that we were unqualified. Detectives must take themselves and their work seriously. A few questions to Harry would have demonstrated that his view of the world was that life was farcical when it was not tragic. I was his pupil.

Our job was to catch store clerks pocketing money that should have gone into the cash register. See *Willmark Service System, Inc. v. Wirtz,* 317 F.2d 486 (1963); *Campbell v. Willmark Service System, Inc.,* 123 F.2d 204 (1941).

We began at 8:30 in the morning in the Willmark office, located in the old Evening Star Building at 11th and Pennsylvania Avenue. Our crew manager gave us impressive-looking certificates proclaiming to all that we were official Willmark detectives. He gave us marked money and a list of stores to shop.

I was to buy (with marked money) such things as two bottles of aspirin, in a Peoples drugstore (later CVS). I was to give the clerk the exact change and leave immediately without waiting for a receipt. Harry was to follow me to the register to observe if the clerk rang up the sale. If the clerk did not, we called in a report to our crew manager. He would come to the store and arrange for an interview with the clerk and do a search for the marked money. He would seek an admission of a theft of a large sum of money. The store then made a claim for reimbursement to its bonding company. The bonding company required that the case be reported to the police. I now see many legal issues connected with this process, including entrapment, coerced confessions, and defamation. I am pleased to say we made no detections during our three-month tour of duty.

Harry and I spent pleasant days wandering in and out of downtown stores using the Willmark service. Our assignment required us to eat at the lunch counters in these stores. One sunny fall day, when we filled up on more ice cream sodas and toasted tuna sandwiches than we could eat, we ordered sandwiches to go. What to do with all the food? We took the sandwiches to nearby Judiciary Square. This was my first look at the outside of a courthouse.

We decided to give the sandwiches away. Our first offers were greeted with suspicion. Eventually people hanging around the park responded and accepted the food. Our Robin Hood game came to an end when we were fired.

We were happy to leave, but we thought of the people in the park, our constituency. We had established an expectation. They relied on us. As a legal matter, we may have been obligated to give thirty days' notice so they could make other arrangements.

SOMEBODY ELSE, NOT ME

There are cases when extraordinary ingenuity is required to extricate a client from his legal problems. When the client is a man of means, frequent strategy meetings take place, attended by the many lawyers participating in the case.

When I was much younger and found myself at such meetings, I observed a pattern. The experienced lawyers around the table were cautious in disclosing their strategy. Their comments were hedged with reservations, conditions and contingencies, the need for more facts, and the fear of burning bridges.

As I listened, I often thought of bold maneuvers that would solve the problem. Although I knew it best to say nothing in experienced company, I could not keep my mouth shut. I would speak up. After I spoke I would look around the room for approval. I saw none. No approval. But no disapproval.

Then one of the group would say the idea might work. Another would say it sounded interesting, but there were elements here and there that must be considered. Someone else would say, "It's your idea, why don't you go with it? Of course it requires some courage to take such a position, but why don't you, you alone, take on that role?" It is an opportunity and you may be just the right person.

Well, my ideas were not so good. In fact they were bad ideas. In addition, they would bring embarrassment to the person connected with them. Gradually it dawned on me that I was placing myself in the role of a fall guy.

The *Random House Historical Dictionary of American Slang* carries a long entry under fall guy. The definition given is a person who takes the blame for the actions of confederates. There are examples of the use of a fall guy in the early gangster movies.

Now when I find myself in a conference room and a young, energetic lawyer speaks up with the perfect solution, I have the common decency to tell him that the idea has already been considered and rejected. Rejected because there may be subtle ethical issues involved. Rejected because the judge in the case would not look favorably upon such an approach. Rejected because it may bring on problems much greater than the ones we now confront.

The person who has the self-evident solution to a complicated problem must ask himself, "Why am I the only brilliant person in the room? Why hasn't someone else claimed credit for this perfect solution?" The answer is that a complicated problem is a game of pickup sticks. One stick cannot be moved without creating a new arrangement of the sticks, requiring a new strategy for extracting the next stick.

Political cases need fall guys. Watergate is the most analyzed case in which desperate remedies in the form of perfect solutions were considered. The Nixon tapes recorded the schemes. It was a time when perfect solutions submitted by young lawyers were adopted on the spot with terrible consequences for all involved.

In Watergate John Dean decided early on he was not going to be Nixon's fall guy. John Mitchell, Nixon's attorney general, remained a fall guy to the very end.

In Iran-Contra Oliver North testified that he knew he was being set up as the fall guy when he heard himself described at a White House news conference as "the only one who knew what was going on."

A song of yesteryear, called "Somebody Else, Not Me," puts the fall guy concept into rhyme. The great Bert Williams talked and sang it in the Ziegfeld Follies of 1919. The accompanying music is slow and mournful, with reliance on oboe solos in the minor chords. I hope you like it.

Now, the circus played our town one day
And three Bengal tigers got away.
The manager in charge came up to me—
And said, my friend, here's your opportunity.
Somebody's got to go and get them cats
Because the tiger man is sick in bed, so he said.
The man who catches them alive
A real hero he's going to be.

I said, yes sir, a wonderful chance for somebody, I agree.
A wonderful opportunity for somebody else, not me.

Cubes with ebony dots
Often lead to cemetery lots.
For instance last night brought on a fight

Which finished up with fists and shots.
I was the furthest from the door.
The others all got there before.
A body on the floor lay dead.
And through the transom someone said:

Somebody's got to stay behind.
Somebody must remain.
So when the officers arrive—
That somebody will explain
Why our dear brother here ain't alive.

Yes, it's a wonderful chance for somebody—
I do agree.
A wonderful opportunity for somebody else, not me.

THE RISE AND FALL OF THE CHAUFFEUR DRIVEN LIMO

Thorstein Veblen (1857–1929) was a satirist who amused himself by identifying in an austere, amusing vocabulary the strategies people use to gain entry into the prestigious and highly reputable, pecuniary leisure class. Thrift has nothing to do with it. The applicant must demonstrate pecuniary respectability by being a big spender, not by being thrifty. In a word, if we don't inherit wealth, we should have the common decency to fake it.

A member of the leisure class must devote himself to conspicuous consumption. "In order to gain and to hold the esteem of men it is not sufficient merely to possess wealth or power. The wealth or power must be put in evidence, for esteem is awarded only on evidence."

Evidence is oversized homes, with teams of paid help. Evidence is first class travel. Evidence is having a chauffeur to drive the limo.

The chauffeur demonstrates his own pecuniary respectability by attribution. His gentleman employer provides the impressive uniform. The gentleman employer will provide in his will a substantial bequest in recognition of years of faithful service and as part of an unspoken employment non-disparagement clause.

There is a distinction between a chauffeur and a driver. Drivers are part-timers from whom one expects no loyalty. Drivers are often retired police officers who know how to park right in front of a No Parking sign. Drivers are paid by the hour and expect to be tipped. Not so with chauffeurs.

A few years ago a story involving limousine drivers made the rounds in New York City. A law firm ran up a substantial unpaid account with its limousine service. Conventional efforts to collect payment were unsuccessful, so the owner of the service decided to pursue unconventional methods. He interviewed his drivers, and he learned from them a number of interesting things that were overheard on the tape. He learned that the lawyers believed the law firm would not survive another year. He also learned things concerning the lawyers' clients, the lawyers' girlfriends, the lawyers' candid comments about judges and other lawyers. Armed with this information, the owner spoke to the law firm administrator. The bill was paid. The law firm did, in fact, go under, leaving numerous other creditors unpaid.

I recall, back in the 1950's, overhearing a conversation between two prominent lawyers who were trying to settle on whose chauffeur would pick up the other and take them both to their club for lunch.

In those days the front of the Metropolitan Club, from 11:30 a.m. to 3:30 p.m., was the place to study experienced, top-of-the-line chauffeurs. The black Cadillac or black Lincoln limos created a temporary limo-lock along H Street, west of 17th.

While the bankers and lawyers were having lunch, the chauffeurs remained close by. A good chauffeur could sit for hours showing no impatience, and then, when the gentleman appeared, the chauffeur brought the limo forward so that the limo and the gentleman intersected at just the right moment.

Ten years ago a chauffeur was the key witness in a case brought against the estate of a wealthy lawyer by distant relatives of the deceased. The chauffeur was the old-fashioned type. He wore a cap and a uniform. He wore white gloves. He was discreet in all respects and he was observant of the gentleman-chauffeur privilege, a privilege as sanctified as the attorney-client privilege.

He had been remembered handsomely in the will. He was now to give evidence to defend the will. He explained to the jury that the gentleman's occasional mental lapses were nothing more than what most elderly people experience. The gentleman was thoughtful and kind to those who served him, as proved by the bequest to the chauffeur. He said that his gentleman had said many times that his relatives never earned a penny by hard work. They would file suit to break the will. They would be envious of what the elderly gentleman bequeathed to his faithful chauffeur. The relatives lost, as well they should have.

A first-class chauffeur had to have the tact of an English butler combined with the experience of the concierge at the Ritz.

These times are not conducive to the retention of a liveried chauffeur. What would the chauffeur drive? Would he get behind the wheel of a utility vehicle, a muddy Land Rover or, worse yet, a tin-plated Hummer? These are the times when people of standing wish to be downwardly mobile. They wear expensive, pre-ripped, pre-torn jeans. You cannot tell a factory second from a top-of-the-line.

Veblen might say that there is a persistent populist working-man strain in American history. That is why the leisure class dress Ralph Lauren-rugged as they stroll the corridors of Home Depot, elegant and shabby, and both at the same time.

LATE THOUGHTS IN
THE AFTERNOON

Should I take my book of business and join up with others who will let me keep more of what I bring in? Would I take a good governmental agency general counsel's position if it were offered?

What is the future of the law practice? As law firms sign on for the business protections that a limited liability partnership gives and as law firms advertise, even using brand names, the law practice in the public mind is indistinguishable from any other business. Is it likely that the government will take the game away from the courts and turn it over to a government agency? Arthur Andersen, before it hit the iceberg, had more lawyers working for it than any law firm in the country. The Securities and Exchange Commission has taken control of the accountants and may branch out and pick up law firms. Or there may be another agency created just for law firms.

Is there a real difference between the mind of an accountant and the mind of a lawyer? Accountants believe everything can be made precise and placed on a balance sheet. What is not in numbers does not exist. That leaves out most of what life is about. Lawyers, when they are thinking straight, know that human conduct is not numerical. It is unpredictable, elusive, contradictory, and often funny.

A lawyer begins to think, how much business have I lost because of conflicts in this big firm? The bigger we get, the more conflicts. There is talk around here of another merger with another big firm. If that happens, I will have more conflict problems.

What about putting all aside and try teaching? I have the impressive academic background. What could I teach? Would I be a good teacher? Teaching would require me to take three months off to bone up, and then I must make up my mind that I would be the best teacher the students ever had. That means throwing myself into it and putting on a two-hour show twice a week. I no longer have the energy it takes.

Are the differences between the types of law practice so well defined that the general designation of lawyer for us all is inapplicable? For instance, the big-firm practice—big transactions and big litigation in the millions—has nothing to do with the small-time practice representing people in trouble (some criminal, some contingent cases, and some other things). There should be different ethical rules for each. One size does not fit all. When a firm representing a big corporation makes a blunder, the big corporation does not complain to bar counsel as an individual client does. The big corporation uses self-help. It fires the firm.

The billing committee wants me to improve my "realization rate." What poet came up with those words, realization rate, the difference between the bills and what the client pays. The billing committee never gives me permission to cut a bill, so I have problems with the realization rate. They would not give me permission to cut a bill for work I did for my sick mother. They were once talking about suing one of my clients to collect a bill.

I recall a law school teacher saying to the class, never sue a client because you'll get a counterclaim for malpractice, and your bills will be scrutinized in such a way that there will be embarrassing disclosures.

I am never so happy as when I get a new client. New people. New documents. New reasons to say to myself (but never to the client), how could he be so dumb? On that point I also say to myself that we have all been as dumb in our own way and we will be in the future. How to deal with people in trouble? It involves who I am and who the client is. I am five different people and so is the client.

The interesting part of practicing law is trying to fit our conduct to our precepts. In order to do that I must first identify my own precepts. Are they fixed or are they changing? I suppose I am like everyone else. I act according to my inclinations and say these are my precepts.

When I drift toward cynicism, as I am now doing, I reread what Piero Calamandrei said. He practiced law in Rome during the 1930s. The courts he practiced in were rumored to be corrupt, and litigation once commenced never ended. Calamandrei was undaunted. Let me read him again.

Who was it that invented that cowardly and temporizing proverb, *Habent sua sidera liter*? Though couched in decorous Latin it says in effect that justice is a game of chance, never to be taken seriously. Surely the expres-

213

sion was coined by some legal hireling without scruples or passion, hoping in some way to excuse his own incompetence, to overcome his remorse, and to lessen his toil. But you, young lawyer, cast aside this epigram of resignation, this enervating drug; burn the page where it is written, and when you take a case that seems just, work fervently with the conviction that by faith in justice you will succeed in changing the course of the stars, regardless of the astrologers.

A client who has gotten himself in real trouble wants to test me to see whether I become judgmental once I know the real bad things he has done. It has been described by a chemistry class word—*titration*, liquid being released drop by drop from a long tube. The client first discloses a minor infraction of the law. He watches to see if there is a reaction. I show no emotion. He tells me of another more serious infraction. Still testing.

I usually have a pretty good idea of what the last drop will be about. Before the next meeting I titrate over to 18 U.S.C. §1001, the false statement statute, and 18 U.S.C. §1512, the obstruction statute, both of which are beloved by prosecutors.

TRUTH, FALSEHOOD, AND THE LAW

Headline cases focus on how the law deals with lying. People lie to conceal something already done. What was done may be illegal, immoral, embarrassing, or any combination of the three. The effort to conceal converts something that may be of no great consequence into something very serious, a felony.

Let us begin with perjury. *Perjury* is defined in two places in title 18 of the United States Code. The first is section 18-1621. This is the general perjury statute.

It is the stating under oath, as a material fact, a lie with the intent to deceive. The government must prove, first, that you were under oath. Second, that what you said was material, that is, of some significance. Third, that you lied and you intended to lie.

How does the government prove that? It does so by a witness who says that what you said was untrue. The testimony of one witness (he said, she said) will not do it. There must be two witnesses or one witness plus corroboration. The corroboration may be in the form of documentary evidence or facts related to your conduct, in addition to what you said under oath.

The general perjury statute picks up many statements that have nothing to do with the government—for instance, testimony in a deposition when you are under oath or in an affidavit.

The second place where *perjury* is defined is section 18-1623. It is grand jury perjury.

The statute says that the crime consists of stating under oath to a grand jury or the court a material fact that is a lie, the same as set forth in section 18-1621. But there is more. The government can prove its case by the testimony of one witness who says you lied. The statute does away with the two-witnesses-or-one-witness-plus-corroboration rule. The government can also prove its case by showing that you made contradictory statements before a grand jury, and the government need not prove which of the statements is true or false. As we see, it is easier for the government to get a conviction if the lying is before a grand jury. Why should this be? There is no good reason except that prosecutors wanted it that way.

There is another statute favored by prosecutors to catch liars. No oath is required. No special corroboration is required. It is the prosecutor's delight. It is the false statement statute, title 18-1001. You will see references to it in the lower left-hand corner of many government documents. It says that signing a document that contains a false statement may be a violation of title 18-1001.

Here is the relevant language:

Sec. 1 001. Statements or entries generally

(a) Except as otherwise provided in this section, whoever, in any matter within the jurisdiction of the executive, legislative, or judicial branch of the Government of the United States, knowingly and willfully—

(1) falsifies, conceals, or covers up by any trick, scheme, or device a material fact;

(2) makes any materially false, fictitious, or fraudulent statement or representation; or

(3) makes or uses any false writing or document knowing the same to contain any materially false, fictitious, or fraudulent statement or entry.

Let's talk more about section 18-1001, a dangerous statute if there ever was one.

The government proves the crime by showing that (1) you made a false statement or concealed something; (2) the statement was material; (3) it was done knowingly and willfully; and (4) you made it directly or indirectly to any branch of the United States government.

The statement need not be written. It need not be under oath. Silence may constitute a false statement if silence is misleading. A statement may be considered a violation even though it is literally true but is misleading.

There need be no transcript of the question asked and the answer given. The testimony of one witness is sufficient to make out the government's case.

When we talk about unpleasant things like lying, we end up with another unpleasant subject, lie detectors.

Lewis Thomas, the distinguished physician and author, says the lie detector gives him hope that the world is all right despite the overwhelming reasons for discouragement. The lie detector proves that we cannot tell a lie, even a small one, without setting off a smoke alarm deep in the brain, resulting in the sudden discharge of nerve impulses and neurohormones. This is recorded by the lie detector gadgetry along with other changes, including in the heart rate and the manner of breathing.

Thomas says this is good news. It proves we are a moral species designed to be truthful to one another. We have evolved beyond guiltless mendacity, as is the case with animals who lie to one another all the time. Biologically speaking, it is healthy for us to stop lying to one another, whenever possible.

WE ARE PLEASED TO
HAVE WITH US ...

Two weeks ago I attended a dinner followed by an after-dinner speech by a man who was introduced as a prominent lawyer. The introduction included his educational background, honors, publications, and general accomplishments. It was needlessly detailed. An ominous sign. A long introduction forecasts a long speech.

The speaker endeavored to make legal ethics both interesting and funny, all with no success. He worked in a few jokes and added stories concerning astonishing cases of conflicts of interest. On and on he went. He began the mechanical platitudes concerning the need to reestablish the honor of the profession. He concluded with a generous offer. He would take questions. I took off and hurried over to the parking lot. It was closed. I took a cab home. On the way I asked myself how even a good speaker cannot hold an audience's attention when listeners can tune out using their mental TV channel changers.

C-SPAN televises after-dinner speeches. That is the way to attend them—at home, seated in a comfortable chair, with a cup of coffee and the channel changer close by. If the speech is a good one, then it is twice as good with no need to stand in line at the hat check counter.

The only after-dinner speaker I wish to see in person is someone who has been bounced around by life and survived to tell about it in no more than 20 minutes tops. I like a speaker who appears to be constructing a familiar essay as he speaks, coloring the events with irony and a respectable apprehension born of life's uncertainties.

That brings me back to George M. Cohan, whom I have mentioned before and I am sure I will mention again. Cohan, in his time, could act better than any dancer, dance better than any actor, sing better than any playwright and write songs better than any singer. In addition, he played the piano by ear. In 1936 President Franklin Roosevelt gave him a Congressional Gold Medal for strengthening the morale of the nation by writing the songs "Over There," "You're a Grand Old Flag," and "Give My Regards to Broadway."

Years ago I heard a recording of after-dinner remarks given by George M. Cohan in acknowledgment of an award he received from the Catholic Actors Guild. Cohan had his joking ways and he began his speech by saying he always wanted to give a good speech but he just didn't have the talent. When he was writing plays he had trouble getting past the first act. He recalled that he was rehearsing the first act of one of his plays when the actors came to him and said they wanted to select wardrobe for the second act. They wanted to know what happens in the second act. Cohan said, "Listen—you tell me what wardrobe you would like to wear in that second act, and I will tell you quite a bit about what happens in the second act." He continued the speech with recollections of his father, a vaudevillian.

I wish I had been there to see and hear the great George M. His speech fulfilled all the criteria of what a good speech should be: It was gently humorous and revealed much about a person who had lived an extraordinary life.

I am on the lookout for old books containing speeches. My collection includes a book of Chauncey Depew's speeches. Quite a name, Chauncey Depew. And it was real. Chauncey Depew (1834–1928) was a railroad lawyer, United States senator, orator, and after-dinner speaker. He continued making speeches well into his 80's. He opened with the story of a speech he made out west to a group of farmers. He told them he was in every respect as sound in mind and body at 80 as he was when he was 40. A farmer stood up and said, "Mr. Depew, when you said you are as sound in mind and body at 80 as you were at 40 it shows that you are of unsound mind."

I also collect books on speech making. I have even read a few of them. They are all about the same. No secrets. My own experience in giving speeches has taught me several things. It is best to write out and read a speech that is to be given on a solemn occasion, such as a memorial or funeral service. What is to be said should be thought through carefully and delivered as written.

An after-dinner or after-lunch speech must be tailored to fit the audience and delivered with an element of spontaneity. No reading. I like to forecast how long I intend to speak by saying, "You will be out of here in ten minutes." Audiences, as defendants, like to know when they are free to leave. They do not like indeterminate sentences.

In my speeches, I enjoy recalling someone the audience and I have known. I supply an anecdote to bring the person to life through some revealing occurrence. Over the years I have met an irregular parade of puzzling, unpredictable, singular people, most of them unknown beyond their own circle of friends and enemies. Several come to mind now. There was Manny A., who practiced law but whose real occupation was studying the vast domain of womanhood. His love affairs were tempestuous and varied. He liked women of the type described in Paul Dresser's song of yesteryear, "My Gal Sal": "a wild sort of devil, but dead on the level was My Gal Sal." There was John F., an outstanding college athlete, an FBI agent, a lawyer, a linguist. He served two prison terms. He was at all times deeply religious and amoral.

And then there was Alimony John J. His pockets were his file cabinet. He refused to read mail that had bad news unless he was comfortably situated in a warm bath.

I could go on, but I must close down. I promised I would have you out of here in ten minutes, and I see by the clock ...

TELL US A STORY

The moviemakers early on discovered that the number of basic plots is limited. You need only fast-forward your DVD player through the movie previews and you will see most of the basic plots speed by, one after another, in the space of five minutes.

In the 1935 play *Boy Meets Girl* a cynical Hollywood writer is talking to an obtuse leading man who cannot follow a simple story line. The writer makes it simple: "Boy meets girl. Boy loses girl. Boy gets girl." The writer says, as an aside, that it is a story that has become the great American fairy tale. It sends the audience back home in a happy frame of mind.

Christopher Booker, in his recent book *The Seven Basic Plots: Why We Tell Stories*, alleges that all stories conform to seven basic plots that have ancient origins and are present in one form or another in all cultures. They appear in the Bible and other religious writings. They are used over and over again in movies, plays, and novels and on HBO.

Booker gives each a name. He begins with what he calls "Overcoming the Monster," the story in which the hero destroys the bad man. See James Bond, *King Kong*, *Jurassic Park*, and *Star Wars*. Next is "Rags to Riches," in which the inconspicuous hero, starting out with nothing, ends up with everything. See Charlie Chaplin in *The Gold Rush* and Dickens' *Great Expectations* and *David Copperfield*. In "The Quest" story, the hero travels a dangerous road in search of hidden treasure. See *Lord of the Rings* and *Raiders of the Lost Ark*. There is the "Voyage and Return" story. See *Robinson Crusoe* and Orson Welles in *The Third Man*.

There is the "Comedy" story of humorous contradictions and mistaken identities. See *The Marriage of Figaro* and the Marx Brothers. In the "Tragedy" story, things don't happen for the best, and the hero, because of a fatal flaw, ends a failure. See *Bonnie and Clyde* and *Anna Karenina*. And finally there is the "Rebirth" story. See Dickens' *A Christmas Carol* and Dostoyevsky's *Crime and Punishment*, in which Raskolnikov faces up to his guilt in murdering the moneylender and commences his own rehabilitation.

Booker says the pattern in each story engages something deep within us. We use the story to translate the irrational chaos that surrounds us into a comforting fiction that says life proceeds on rational lines, and good generally prevails over evil.

Booker says each basic plot involves conflict. Lawyers are experts on conflict. We live the adversary system. One against the other. This raised a question in my mind as to what the basic legal plots are. Why do people litigate?

To get the answer I called a friend who spent the last thirty years trying high-intensity cases of all kinds. He took a detached and, I would say, amusing cynical stance. He came up with this evaluation of the basic legal plots, the reasons people involve themselves in lawsuits: greed, 60 percent; vindictiveness, 15 percent; irrationality, 10 percent; desperation, 10 percent; and an honest misunderstanding, 5 percent.

He said lawyers get a distorted view of greed because most litigants want the lawyer to get them money or to protect them from someone else's getting their money. All this talk about who gets the money leads lawyers into believing that everybody does nothing but think about money.

He said greed lurks in the subjects taught in law school. As an example, the law of contracts. The elements of an enforceable contract can be put in one volume. Why does a leading text on contracts run to thirty volumes? It is because all the cases discussed are about the way greedy people try to get an advantage. Greed figures in wills and estates. The survivors, who earned none of the money in the estate, fight, as a matter of principle, to the last dollar.

My friend closed by saying that in many of his cases the lawyers were the only honorable people connected with the dispute. It comes back to the statement that the lawyer is never as bad as his client wants him to be.

There are two other basic legal plots I wish to mention. One involves a type who often finds his way to a lawyer's office. A schemer. He enjoys being alone in the world to exploit the opportunities that come his way or that he develops as he moves from one scheme to another. He needs legal advice because he has trouble marking off the difference between right and wrong. Greed for money is not his consuming interest. His wish is to use his ingenuity. One writer has labeled such a type as an adventurer in capitalism.

225

The other basic legal plot, the one that redeems it all, is where the lawyer corrects an injustice. It is one of life's great moments. It is, to use Booker's words, overcoming the monster, defeating the bully.

Lawyers use stories as a dramatist does. The trial is a play based on a dramatic story line that the lawyer extracts from his client's recitation of names, dates, places, documents, impressions, and accusations. The story line, once settled on, determines what is relevant and what is irrelevant. This requires judgment of a high order. It determines the opening statement, the witnesses to be called, and the closing argument.

The story ends the old-fashioned way, like a well-made play. The jury renders its verdict and the curtain falls.

PEOPLE

Edgar Lee Masters (1869–1950) was a partner of Clarence Darrow's in their practice of law in Chicago. Masters was successful as a lawyer and he had energy to spare. He wrote the poems entitled Spoon River Anthology, published in 1915. The poems are epitaphs in free verse. Masters used the small-town people he knew growing up as his inspirations.

Spoon River Anthology made Masters famous. He discontinued his law practice (he and Darrow had a falling out), and he moved to New York to spend his time as a writer.

State's Attorney Fallas

I, the scourge-wielder, balance-wrecker,
Smiter with whips and swords;
I, hater of the breakers of the law;
I, legalist, inexorable and bitter,
Driving the jury to hang the madman, Barry Holden,
Was made as one dead by light too bright for eyes,
And woke to face a Truth with bloody brow:
Steel forceps fumbled by a doctor's hand
Against my boy's head as he entered life
Made him an idiot.
I turned to books of science
To care for him.
That's how the world of those whose minds are sick
Became my work in life, and all my world.
Poor ruined boy! You were, at last, the potter
And I and all my deeds of charity
The vessels of your hand.

Edgar Lee Masters

John M. Church

I was attorney for the "Q"
And the Indemnity Company which insured
The owners of the mine.
I pulled the wires with judge and jury,
And the upper courts, to beat the claims
Of the crippled, the widow and orphan,
And made a fortune thereat.

The bar association sang my praises
In a high-flown resolution.
And the floral tributes were many—
But the rats devoured my heart
And a snake made a nest in my skull!

Edgar Lee Masters

Granville Calhoun

I wanted to be County Judge
One more term, so as to round out a service
Of thirty years.
But my friends left me and joined my enemies,
And they elected a new man.
Then a spirit of revenge seized me,
And I infected my four sons with it,
And I brooded upon retaliation,
Until the great physician, Nature,
Smote me through with paralysis
To give my soul and body a rest.
Did my sons get power and money?
Did they serve the people or yoke them,
To till and harvest fields of self?
For how could they ever forget
My face at my bed-room window,
Sitting helpless amid my golden cages
Of singing canaries,
Looking at the old court-house?

Edgar Lee Masters

Henry C. Calhoun

I reached the highest place in Spoon River,
But through what bitterness of spirit!
The face of my father, sitting speechless,
Child-like, watching his canaries,
And looking at the court-house window
Of the county judge's room,
And his admonitions to me to seek
My own in life, and punish Spoon River
To avenge the wrong the people did him,
Filled me with furious energy
To seek for wealth and seek for power.
But what did he do but send me along
The path that leads to the grove of the Furies?
I followed the path and I tell you this:
On the way to the grove you'll pass the Fates,
Shadow-eyed, bent over their weaving.
Stop for a moment, and if you see
The thread of revenge leap out of the shuttle
Then quickly snatch from Atropos
The shears and cut it, lest your sons,
And the children of them and their children
Wear the envenomed robe.

Edgar Lee Masters

WHO TO BELIEVE,
WHO NOT TO BELIEVE

We have reason to believe that playing the law game gives us a skill, perhaps an intuition, that tells us whether the person we happen to be dealing with is on the level, whether he is trying to deceive us. Some people are better at it than others.

Those who deal with big events, people such as Winston Churchill and Harry Truman, could not have climbed so high without a way-above-average skill in knowing who to believe and who not to believe. Even they could be fooled.

There were certain events that took place in July 1945 in Potsdam, a suburb of Berlin, Germany, that make the point. Winston Churchill and Harry Truman were meeting with Joseph Stalin. Germany had just surrendered. The war against Japan continued. Churchill and Truman wanted a firm commitment from Stalin that Russia would declare war on Japan and join with the Allies in the Japanese invasion. In exchange Stalin wanted new boundaries favorable to Russia.

Churchill, in volume six of his history of the Second World War, describes what happened. At the outset Joseph Stalin gave his unqualified commitment that Russia was ready to declare war against Japan and provide troops as needed. He then turned to his own wish list.

The meeting and the world changed when Secretary of War Henry Stimson handed Churchill a sheet of paper on which was written "Babies satisfactorily born." Stimson said the words meant the atomic bomb had just been tested and it was a reality. The next day they received a detailed description of the explosion and its unequaled destructive power. The Russians were no longer needed. The negotiating leverage had shifted. The war would be over without Russia's help.

Churchill and Truman had to decide what to say to Stalin. They were certain that the atomic bomb project was a closely held secret unknown to the Russians. Stalin must be told something. It would not sit well for him to learn of it days later when Japan was to be given an ultimatum. Should it be in writing or by word of mouth? Should it be at a formal and special meeting or in the course of the daily conferences, or after the meetings?

Truman thought it best to give the word in an informal way by describing the atomic bomb as an entirely novel form of bomb that would have a decisive effect on Japan's willingness to continue the war. Say nothing more, nothing less.

As the Potsdam meeting drew to its close (after some significant drinking), Churchill watched as Truman approached Stalin. The two spoke to each other through their interpreters.

Here is Churchill describing what he saw: "I was perhaps five yards away, and I watched with the closest attention the momentous talk. I knew what the President was going to do.

What was vital to measure was its effect on Stalin. I can see it all as if it were yesterday. He seemed to be delighted."

Churchill and Truman were convinced that Stalin had no idea of the significance of what he was being told. Churchill wrote, "If he had had the slightest idea of the revolution in world affairs which was in progress, his reactions would have been obvious. Nothing would have been easier than for him to say, thank you so much for telling me about your new bomb. I of course have no technical knowledge. May I send my expert in these nuclear sciences to see your expert tomorrow morning?"

What if Stalin did in fact know all about the atomic bomb project and knew of the test? What if beforehand he had spoken with his advisers concerning what to say if he were told about the atomic bomb? How should he react? He certainly would not want to give away his own secret knowledge. The best way to deal with it would be to mislead by passing it off with a casual comment of his own.

The fact of the matter is that Stalin knew about the atomic bomb project even before Harry Truman. Truman, as vice president, knew nothing about it until one month after President Roosevelt's death on April 12, 1945.

The disclosures that have come to light within the past fifty years confirm that the Kremlin received top-secret information concerning the atomic bomb project as early as 1942.

Klaus Fuchs (1911–1988) was a physicist who was born in Germany, left Germany and went to England, and became a British citizen. In 1942 he worked in England on what became the atomic bomb project. In 1943 the British sent him to the United States to continue with the project. He was present when the first bomb exploded.

Fuchs confessed to the British secret service on January 24, 1950, that he began spying for the Russians as early as 1942.

His trial lasted only an hour and a half. The indictment did not mention that Fuchs admitted committing espionage from 1942 through 1949. When asked to enter his plea, Fuchs stated he was guilty and that he hoped his confession would mitigate his wrongdoing.

There was no jury. The only witness was the person who took Fuchs' confession. A full trial would have been a great embarrassment to the British, who had ignored early warnings that Fuchs was not to be trusted. There were even rumors that people at the very top of the British secret service had protected Fuchs.

Fuchs was sentenced to fourteen years.

In his written confession Fuchs said he passed to Russia all the information he had. He commented on his own state of mind. One compartment consisted of his personal relations with friends. With them he wished to be honorable and helpful. In the other compartment he was a spy, on his own, independent of the society within which he worked. Each compartment was closed to the other. "Looking back at it now the best way of expressing it seems to be to call it a controlled schizophrenia.

A DOMESTIC
RELATIONS MAN

Some years ago I represented a woman I shall call Mrs. Corelli, in a contested divorce case. I fix the time as 1955. Mr. Corelli was represented by Jean Boardman.

Jean Boardman was a leader of the local domestic relations bar. He was there for either the husband or the wife in the cases involving prominent members of Washington society. Although I had never met him, I often saw him walking near 15th and H streets, near the Shoreham Building, where his office was located. His erect posture, his long strides, and his habit of humming and singing to himself as he strode along drew the attention of the passersby. It was through the Corelli divorce that I met and got to know Boardman.

He paid me the honor of dropping by my office one afternoon to discuss settlement. In the course of the discussion I pressed my client's case strongly, and suggested that Boardman was representing an unworthy client.

Boardman invited me to calm down. He said that if by chance Mr. Corelli, the party who had the money, had hired me instead of Mrs. Corelli, I would be carrying on in the identical immature manner but it would be for Mr. Corelli. He added that if the Corelli case was tried instead of settled, I was in for a few surprises. The good sense of what he said made a lasting impression.

As it turned out, the case was tried and I was very much surprised to find that my client had concealed from me a key document.

Thereafter, when I saw Boardman striding up and down 15th Street, I walked along with him. I learned that he had come to Washington from the Midwest, employed as a stenographer and secretary to a congressman. Boardman's real love was singing. He had wished to take voice training, but it never worked out. While working for the congressman he went to law school. In a relatively short time he built up a very active divorce practice, and by 1955 he was one of a small group who were offered the best divorce litigation.

I learned also that in a field of practice where the truth is the first casualty, he had established a reputation as a man of unique reliability. He was not a religious man, as far as I could tell, but he was honest by instinct and habit. Judges knew they could take him at his word.

In time we became friends. I saw him often at the courthouse. Here, too, he was in constant motion. He paced the corridors while waiting for his case to be called. As time permitted, he studied looseleaf notebooks he had compiled containing his research into the field of American popular music from the 1890's to the 1940's. He spent free time in the music division of the

Congressional Library, examining old sheet music and copyright records. He knew the details of the lives of many of the early popular songwriters.

Boardman was one of the founding members of the Barbershop Singing Society and he sang with several of its groups. He knew the lyrics of hundreds of old songs. He was at his happiest singing in his rich baritone voice songs such as "After the Ball Is Over" and "Sweet Adeline."

Once his case was called, there was even more animation. He fingered documents. He opened law books. He gestured. He paced. Each question from the court was responded to with an engaging bluntness. An expert typist, he did all his own typing. I saw him on a number of occasions sit down at his typewriter and bang out agreements, papers, and pleadings. He was remarkably brief and very persuasive. In fact, in one case he convinced a judge in the domestic relations branch of the court to give his client a jury trial. Domestic relations cases were always non-jury. It is set forth in *Rodenberg* v. *Rodenberg*, 213 A.2d 510 (D.C. 1965). I am told by a knowledgeable practitioner that Boardman is the only lawyer to have accomplished the feat.

Because of his fine reputation, he was often asked by those seeking judgeships to write letters of recommendation. He routinely refused. He said that on one occasion a defeated congressman's aide had asked for such a letter. Boardman said he kept to his resolution of writing no letters, but as he told the story, he did promise that if the gentleman was appointed to the court, he would do the newly appointed judge a favor. He would personally help him find his way to the courthouse.

The last time I saw Boardman he was striding up 15th Street. We chatted, and he told me this story as we walked along, with me a step or two behind. One of his clients, a wealthy widower, was frequently sued for causes sounding in breach of promise by women who produced at trial incriminatory letters. Boardman advised the gentleman not to compose sweetheart letters. The gentleman said he would follow the advice, but he didn't keep his word. He continued to write letters to his lady friends, addressing them as "My dear Helen," or "Dear Ruth," or whoever his love of the moment was, but he always added "and Ladies and Gentlemen of the Jury."

Just as I wrote out that recollection I recalled some other advice that domestic relations specialists of years ago liked to give to their clients: "Do right and fear no man. Don't write and fear no woman." You don't hear talk like that anymore. Most states have banned by statute the breach-of-promise suit. It is probably wise legislation, but it withdrew from the practice some interesting litigation.

A FORENSIC FABLE

Let us call him Jack Davis. Jack's main client was a collection agency that sent him hundreds of cases each month. Jack sent out strong dunning letters to the debtors and, if necessary, filed lawsuits.

Jack's office was chaos. He covered his desk with files, papers, letters, pleadings, books, coffee cups, clocks, giveaway calendars, and notebooks. The office floor duplicated the desk, with the additional clutter of unopened pocket parts of *Corpus Juris Secundum*.

Jack worked in spasms of activity followed by paralysis. In his manic phase he screamed at debtors on the phone, signed nasty letters, drafted pleadings, and looked through the new files as he tossed around the clutter on his desk.

He never let clients or visiting lawyers see him in his office. Jack had an adjacent office for such meetings. It had a clean desk, two leather chairs, and books well placed in an impressive bookcase. The radio was tuned to the classical music station. It was the office of the well-organized man in full control.

Jack said that when he went to see a lawyer and the lawyer had a clean desk, it intimidated him. It was the office of a man who had everything in order. He concentrated on just one thing at a time. He was not a man to be trifled with. A desk covered with papers signals procrastination, distraction, confusion, unfiled papers, statutes running, appointments missed.

There is much to be said for the person who works with a clean desk. When he leaves his office at 5:30, his desk is clean; he has completed his billing records and has made his diary entries.

Nevertheless there is a case to be made for disorder. Justice Felix Frankfurter was once quoted as saying, "I don't like a man to be too efficient. He's likely to be not human enough."

Two people who thrived on disorder were Franklin D. Roosevelt and Winston Churchill. Those who met with FDR saw a desk covered with papers, notes, opened and unopened letters, souvenirs, ship models, small statues, straight pens, and fountain pens. Raymond Moley, an FDR New Dealer, said, "To look upon [Roosevelt's] policies as the result of a unified plan was to believe that the accumulation of stuffed snakes, baseball pictures, school flags, old tennis shoes, carpenter's tools, geometry books, and chemistry sets in a boy's bedroom could have been put there by an interior decorator."

FDR delighted in his contradictions. In 1945, when he was preparing for his fourth term as president, he convinced James Byrnes, William Douglas, Robert Jackson, and others that each was to be his choice, Roosevelt's choice, as vice president. He mentioned to none of them the name of Harry Truman, the person who turned out to be his selection.

FDR's companion in arms, Winston Churchill, did not get out of bed until noon. When he awoke in the morning, he went through the morning newspapers with a big scissors, cutting out what he wanted to use. Then he had breakfast. Then he was given the confidential-cable box containing the things that needed immediate attention. As he took them out, he scribbled side comments. When he wished to write a letter or a memorandum, he dictated it to the nearby secretary, who typed as he spoke. No shorthand. He liked dictating directly to the typist. Churchill did not work from a clean desk. There was no desk. Add to that arrangement a cigar and some sipping whiskey.

When Jack seated himself in his executive chair in the adjacent office with the clean desk in front of him, he knew he was meant for better things than a hectic collection practice. One of these days, when he had enough money, he would go to a small town in the West, Arizona or Colorado. He would establish himself there and run for office. He would do something worthwhile. He would redeem himself for all those threatening letters he sent out and those threatening telephone conversations. He would expose those credit card companies that drive poor people into bankruptcy. He would run on the reform ticket. With this daydream in mind, he took in an associate and gradually turned over the practice to him.

Morton, for that was the associate's first name, was different from Jack. Morton saw something in the collection practice that Jack did not see. Morton put an end to threatening letters. Morton worked out reasonable settlements. Few cases ever went to trial.

Morton did not take a default judgment against a debtor who didn't appear. He got in touch with the debtor and offered a compromise of the claim. Lawyers representing debtors who did not know Morton were surprised at how accommodating he was.

The judges who presided over the small claims court relied on Morton to settle his own cases and most of the other cases where debtors were unrepresented by counsel. One judge called Morton "the Saint of the Small Claims Court." Morton, at the end of his working day, had the satisfaction of knowing that he had helped people.

Word came back that Jack had settled in a small Colorado town and had run for some municipal office. His opponent spread the word that Jack was a nasty collection lawyer. Jack lost and was not heard from again.

Morton placed a rocking chair in the adjacent, clean-desk office. When he felt he needed to collect his thoughts, he rocked away and reflected on his good fortune.

The moral:

The bird with feathers of blue

Is waiting for you

Back in your own backyard.

A MATTER OF STYLE

An actor who plays the part of a lawyer on TV or in the movies has only a few stock character parts to select from. There is Clarence Darrow, with the suspenders, the tousled hair, the necktie askew, the country slyness. See Spencer Tracy in *Inherit the Wind*.

There is the big-time well-dressed litigator with juniors trailing behind him, prepared with documents to corroborate whatever he says. See James Mason in *The Verdict*. See Paul Newman in the same movie playing the desperate loner, underfinanced, aligned with a good cause, representing the underdog.

There is the dead-earnest cross-examiner who sees into the soul of the lying witness. See Raymond Burr as Perry Mason. See Charles Laughton doing the same thing in *Witness for the Prosecution*.

There is Gregory Peck as the virtuous, honorable Atticus Finch in *To Kill a Mockingbird*. And see Peck again in *The Paradine Case*. This fellow Gregory Peck seems to have had quite a law practice.

John Mortimer came up with a new style, the resourceful, ironic, puncturer-of-the-pompous *Rumpole of the Bailey.*

The stock characters for women lawyers include the woman who is efficient, witty, professional, intelligent, and most of the time all business. See Rosalind Russell. There is the woman who says little, but when she speaks she identifies the point everyone missed.

Most practicing lawyers fit into one of the stock types. There are, however, one-of-a-kind exceptions. I would like to sketch in two I have known.

First, there is Ben R. When I worked with him, he had a client with a large profitable business that was burdened with regulatory problems. The client made no serious business decisions without consulting Ben. These consultations commenced with the client giving a summary of the problem. Ben then repeated it, mixing up the dates, mispronouncing names, and forgetting who said what to whom. Ben finished few sentences. Any legal opinion was instantly qualified by subjective views of judges, lawyers, witnesses, and sometimes weather conditions.

Floating on this Nile of talk were headnotes of cases, eulogies, government regulations, confidential disclosures from undisclosed sources, and speculations about what the Federal Trade Commission, the Department of Justice, or the euro might do.

Add to that a dash of mysticism and you have it. When Ben finished off his Barber of Seville recitation, he lit up a cigar. The client took from it what he wanted and usually it turned out well.

Is there an explanation for Ben's success? I think there is. Ben had freed himself from the iron grip of rationality, cause and effect, logical deduction, the syllogism (all men are mortal, Socrates is a man ...). He connected with the wisdom of the irrational that places its faith in hunches, instinct, signs, astonishing coincidences, telepathy (mind communicating with mind), and *déjà vu.*

The client had found the best legal minds helpful in the day-to-day legal matters but unsatisfactory when it came to the big decisions. Too logical, too cold, too legal.

He liked Ben because Ben was not in the business of stepping back and logically analyzing the facts and law. Ben got inside the facts themselves. His seemingly incoherent discourse was a narration of what he felt as he cruised around inside the overlapping and contradicting variables of his client's problem.

Neurologists tell us the brain is not the only part of the body that makes decisions. The spinal cord, the stomach, and even the lower intestine have a right to speak. One might say that Ben spoke up for the client's stomach.

Ben was the lawyer for most of the people in the particular industry in which he practiced. He was treated as a living archive of the anecdotal history of the business. The subject of conflicts never came up. This left him free to settle disputes and thwart litigation by a diplomatic use of confidential gossip.

Next up is Herman Miller, the sage of the Landlord and Tenant Court. He was five feet four and weighed in at a good 200 pounds. His clients were real estate companies that managed properties, mostly apartments. Herman spent every morning in L&T commencing at 9:30. The clerk read off the names of those Herman had sued for possession, sometimes a list of fifty names. If no tenant responded, Herman said one word—"Judgment."

When he was not announcing "Judgment" he was reading a novel. There was one landlord and tenant judge who played a game with Herman. It went like this:

Judge to tenant in default on the rent: You say you have lived in that apartment ten years and you paid rent all that time?

Tenant: Yes.

Judge to Miller: Mr. Miller, this tenant has bought that apartment ten times over. I instruct you to give her a deed.

Miller: Your Honor, I have no authority to do that. However, we will certainly take it under advisement, and in the meantime we give the tenant forty-five days extra to make up the rent.

Herman took few vacations. When he did he went to pre-Castro Havana when Havana was called the "Paris of the Caribbean." Herman returned with stories as remarkable as those Marco Polo reported to his friends in Venice.

BUYER BEWARE

An experienced negotiator sets traps for his adversary. One such trap is to declare that something is non-negotiable. This creates a belief that the something has unique value.

A rug dealer sees a customer look at a carpet, walk away, and later casually ask, "What is the price on that rug over there?" The rug dealer is trained to look for the glint in the eye that says, I must have that carpet. If the glint is there, he tells the customer the carpet is not for sale. Non-negotiable. The price is doubled.

A husband foresees that the marriage is not working and he will have to file for divorce. He wants to keep the racing-green sports car. He tells his wife that he will never give up his right to use the beach house. It is non-negotiable. Eventually he gives in. He gives up his right to use the beach house, but he gets the green sports car.

Recently there appeared in the newspapers the obituary of a woman we'll call Helen. She lived a colorful life. From small beginnings she became famous. She married a wealthy man we'll call William. He was an art collector of museum-quality paintings. William had fallem in love with someone else. William decided before his wife learned he had a girlfriend that the Utrillo in his collection was a painting he would never part with.

A year later William's attentions to the other woman became public. A nasty divorce case followed. There were day and night negotiations between the lawyers. Finally the outlines of a settlement were reached. It was then that Helen decided to take charge. She instructed her lawyer to tell the other side that she wanted the Utrillo. She must teach him a lesson. This was one time when he would not get his way.

The demand for the Utrillo produced a deadlock. William would not part with it.

He would rather go to court. Helen's lawyer urged her to give up on the Utrillo and demand another painting. She could get a painting of much greater value. What was on the table was more than she would get if a judge were to decide the case.

Helen rejected her lawyer's advice. It was a matter of principle. If the case had to go to court, so be it.

After much discussion her husband surrendered. Helen got the Utrillo. She had the satisfaction of seeing her husband give up something he never wanted to part with.

Years later, when William died, the IRS reevaluated his estate, including the Utrillo. The experts came to Helen's apartment and eyeballed it. They left and said they needed a Utrillo expert. Utrillos are easy to copy. There are many fake Utrillos around. The experts filed their report. The Utrillo is a good fake.

Helen was angry. He got the best of her. She consulted a lawyer friend who knew her well and also knew William. What should she do? She has been defrauded. The lawyer reviews the property settlement. As he expected, it contains the New York waiver clause. She agreed in writing to waive all claims even those allegedly fraudulently induced. They know how to do these things in New York.

Even if she got by the New York waiver, she could not prove William knew the Utrillo was a fake. Her lawyer said, "Helen, you and I know you knew William was a fake and a fraud. You knew that when you married him. You wanted something he had, a high-living, chauffeur-driven lifestyle. You got it, and when it was over you got a good settlement and the Miami beach house.

"Furthermore, in a fraud case against the estate, the defense would be that you were contributorily negligent. You knew you were dealing with a con man. You should not have accepted at face value anything he said. Nobody else who knew him would."

The lawyer encouraged Helen to get another Utrillo opinion. Many so-called art experts are themselves fakes. The best proof of that is the Han van Meegeren case. He was the Dutch painter who, after the war, was charged with selling to Adolph Hitler's cohort, Hermann Goering, a Vermeer. The Dutch charged van Meegeren with selling a national treasure to a Nazi. He faced the death penalty. Van Meegeren admitted he sold the painting to Goering, but he said he tricked him. The Vermeer was a forgery. And what's more, van Meegeren was the forger.

The prosecutor was not buying it. He had the leading Vermeer expert authenticate the painting. Van Meegeren offered to prove two things. First, the Vermeer expert was a fraud, and second, he, van Meegeren, could paint a Vermeer.

Van Meegeren demanded that the prosecutor suspend the prosecution and deliver to him paints, brushes, turpentine, and other requirements. Van Meegeren, in full view of the prosecutor and the expert, painted a Vermeer. The Vermeer expert was discredited. Van Meegeren pleaded guilty to the lesser crime of forgery and was sentenced only to a year. He died shortly after the trial.

Helen sold her Utrillo to an expert who agreed to pay Helen half of the sales price if he sold it as a true Utrillo. He later got experts to declare it was probably a real Utrillo. William got his way and Helen got her way. Both wonderful people.

DANIEL WEBSTER'S LAST CASE AND FRANK WALSH

T his is being written with Daniel Webster (1782–1852) at my side. Or better put, I am sitting on the marble base of Daniel Webster's statue near Scott Circle at 16th and Massachusetts Avenue. The bronze statue is more than life-size. Webster stands erect like the great orator he was. He has a book in his right hand. He is holding his flowing cape in his left hand. The statue occupies a small park of its own, here in Washington.

Webster's biographer, Robert E. Remini, opens the biography with this description of Webster (picking up bits and pieces from another biography and Stephen Vincent Benét's *The Devil and Daniel Webster*):

> That voice. It mesmerized. It dazzled. And it rang out like a trumpet. Never shrill, never unpleasantly loud, but deep, dark, with a roll of thunder in it, tempered by a richness of tone and powered by a massive chest that sent it hurtling great distances, even in the open

air, it turned "on the harps of the blessed" and shook "the earth underground." Under perfect control, it never broke however high it was driven to convey an emotion or emphasize a point. For a typical three-, four-, or even five-hour oration it usually needed some form of lubrication to be fired up and ready to perform. But once it started to function, it sang out like music in clear and sonorous cadences and swelled and diminished on command. Nobody who heard it ever forgot it. One carried the sound of it to the grave.

And that look. It hypnotized. It riveted. It could wither miscreants with a single glance. Large, deep-socketed black eyes peered out from a "precipice of brows" and glowed like coals in a furnace waiting for the annoyance or offense that would bring them to full heat.

Webster, after graduation from Dartmouth College, obtained admission to the bar by working in a law office. He set up a local solo practice in New Hampshire where he developed a thriving clientele. In time he moved to Boston and entered politics, siding with the Whigs. He was elected to the United States House of Representatives, and then the Senate, where he became its leader and, in the opinion of his contemporaries, its most impressive orator:

He usually began his speeches slowly and quietly, sometimes with long introductions to prepare the ground and capture the undivided attention of his audience. He knew of course that his appearance—

254

bushy eyebrows, deep-set eyes, dark complexion—
and most especially his magnificent voice could
produce within the first half hour a hypnotic effect
on his listeners. But once he entered the main theme
of his address, "all his faculties expand or take on a
new character. His large black eye dilates and kindles
... his voice ranges through all its powerful notes ...
and his gestures, frequent and sometimes violent, are
accompanied with a forward fling of his body which is
more emphatic than graceful." His words then reveal a
"lethal intent." His scorn, his retort, his recrimination
"are hurled upon their object with a deadly skill and
unsparingness almost fiendish." His smile during an
oration could be "angelical," his sneer "diabolical."

New York Mirror, October 1, 1831

He made three efforts to get his party's presidential nomi-
nation. He lost his party's favor by voting in favor of fugitive slave
legislation. He also had a reputation for favoring the big business
interests. His efforts to reconcile the North and the South, to
avoid a secession, proved futile.

In 1840 President William Henry Harrison nominated
him as secretary of state. In 1850 President Millard Fillmore re-
appointed him secretary of state.

In 1852, Mr. Charles Goodyear, for whom the Goodyear
Tire and Rubber Company was later renamed, retained Webster to plead a Goodyear patent case before the Supreme Court.
Webster got $10,000 up front, and $5,000 more if he won, and he
did win. No man, while still holding the position of secretary of
state, had ever before taken a fee and argued a client's case before

the Supreme Court. Webster was aware that this was a controversial matter, but he told his friends he needed the money.

★★★

Now we turn our attention to a spring morning in 1960 and to Frank Walsh. Frank was an elegant gentleman, with a Princeton/Harvard background. He tired of the uptown 15th Street civil practice where the well-known firms were located.

He liked the criminal practice around the courthouse on Fifth Street. It was where one met (as he put it) the big parade, the bondsmen, the detectives, the prosecutors, the has-beens who never were, and many good lawyers. There was (and is) a plaque on the front of a small office building at Fifth and D streets, N.W., identifying it as the place where Daniel Webster had his office. Frank Walsh had his office in that building.

On that 1960 spring morning Frank was getting ready to walk across Fifth Street to the police court when a man walked into the building and saw Frank in the hallway with his briefcase.

From now on I tell the story as Frank told it, many times. This man walks in, sees me, and asks if Daniel Webster is in.

I gave him an ambiguous response. I then asked him what I could do for him. He said he had been arrested for driving while drunk. I asked him if he had any priors. Had he ever been arrested before for drunk driving? He said no.

I asked him if anybody got hurt and he said no. I then knew I could get the DUI knocked down to excessive speed.

He asked what it would cost. I said three hundred dollars. He took out a small checkbook and started writing a check to Daniel Webster. I said Daniel Webster likes cash up front. He counted out the three hundred dollars. I took it and walked across the street to the police court and worked things out.

Now this fellow Daniel Webster, I understand he was a pretty good lawyer in the Supreme Court. We all know that. Big cases, the Dartmouth College case and *McCulloch* v. *Maryland*.

And I am happy to report that he was also pretty good in his last appearance, which just happened to be in the police court.

FRANK WALDROP
IS CALLING

AWashington lawyer in the forties and early fifties would pay attention if he saw that Frank Waldrop had called. Frank Waldrop was the editor-in-chief of the *Times-Herald*, a large-circulation daily newspaper. It was the rowdiest of Washington's four dailies.

Now let's return to Waldrop's telephone call. Waldrop could make a lawyer's career. Frequent favorable mentions and front-page pictures bring in the clients.

Waldrop liked lawyers. He had many close friendships in the local bar. In those days there was the uptown bar, which located itself along 15th Street, and the Fifth Street courthouse bar. The 15th Street lawyers' focus was well-paying civil work. They did little or no criminal work. When they got a bite concerning a criminal case, a corporate executive picked up on a driving-while-drunk charge, they sent it down to the boys on Fifth Street.

Occasionally the *Times-Herald* was the target of a defamation suit. When this happened, Waldrop hired his 15th Street lawyer, William E. Leahy. Leahy in his time was the most successful trial lawyer in Washington.

In one of the *Times-Herald* editions, its columnist, Drew Pearson, accused General Douglas MacArthur of proposing nineteen-gun salutes for friends and "pulling wires" to further his own ambitions. The general wanted $750,000 as fair compensation for injury to his reputation.

The case was never tried. While it was pending, there was a knock on the door of Drew Pearson's Georgetown residence. Fate sent Pearson and the *Times-Herald* a perfect defense in the form of a beautiful Eurasian woman. She had bolted from the Chastleton Apartments at 16th and R streets N.W., where she had been sequestered by the general. She placed in Pearson's hands a collection of General MacArthur's love letters to her. Shortly thereafter, the general's lawyer was made aware that Drew Pearson possessed interesting documents. The lawsuit was dropped. The letters remain unpublished. Although Waldrop disliked being sued, he enjoyed the give-and-take of the litigation process.

Waldrop's name appears, from time to time, as a reliable source in current biographies of public figures. He'll then receive a visit from someone who wishes to conduct an oral history interview. He delivers up in a pleasant Tennessee accent selections from a well-stocked memory decorated by the experiences of a long and interesting life.

His recall of names, dates, and places is astonishing. In the course of an interview, the questioner learns he was born in Tennessee in 1905. He joined the Army in 1925 as an enlisted man. He got into West Point through a competitive examination. After his years at West Point he became a journalist, working for Hearst's *New York Evening Journal*. His newspaper work eventually brought him in the 1930s to the *Times-Herald*. As its editor he had access to influential politicians, local judges, chiefs of police, and military brass.

Each of President Kennedy's biographies includes anecdotes concerning Waldrop's hiring of Jacqueline Bouvier as the *Times-Herald* inquiring photographer. He warned her against getting too involved with that young John Kennedy person. She did not take his advice.

Waldrop has a special interest in those with a touch of the fanatical. He knew Huey Long. He knew Westbrook Pegler. He reported on the rise and fall of many who sincerely believed they had a selfless interest in helping others see the light and this qualification should be recognized by the electorate.

Waldrop's definition of politics is the art of getting money from the rich and votes from the poor on the pretext of protecting one from the other.

Waldrop also made a study of the Washington bureaucrat. Most of the research centered around the career of J. Edgar Hoover. He formed a friendship with Hoover in Hoover's earliest days as a minor governmental clerk. Waldrop maintained that friendship over Hoover's entire astonishing career. At one time, Waldrop contemplated writing a biography of Hoover, using Hoover's career to get at the very root of the concept of the bureaucrat. According to Waldrop's research, Hoover was asked by each president he served to do highly questionable things. Hoover only carried out such requests if the request was put in writing. Thus, if things went wrong, he would take out the writing, point to the name of the author, and tell the posse to go thataway. Hoover's file drawer of written orders and requests made it difficult to turn him out.

Waldrop's journalistic career in Washington, D.C., and his many years as a student of human nature account for his autumnal views. His original robust faith in the rectitude of human nature and the purity of human motives has been chastened into a genial cynicism that adds to the charm of his conversation.

HOW TO MEET
INTERESTING PEOPLE

We may meet interesting people in a bar, on a train, sitting on a park bench, or walking the dog. There is another way to meet interesting people—working as a comrade in arms with co-counsel defending a murder case.

In 1965 Dovey Roundtree, Jean Dwyer, and I each represented a defendant in such a case. The defendants were charged with shooting and killing a one-time friend of theirs. Although Dovey, Jean, and I were acquainted before the trial, each of us looked forward to working together at counsel table.

They both, despite the difficulties women had 35 years ago establishing a place at the trial bar, were successful and competent criminal lawyers. Each started out trying court-appointed criminal cases when there was no money to pay them. They put their talent on display when wit, optimism, and luck were much more important than a course in advanced criminal procedure. In time they attracted lots of paying clients.

My client instructed me to enter an insanity defense. This meant that he would not take the stand. There is a platitude in the law that the defendant who asserts an insanity defense does not testify. Even when the defendant suffers from a serious mental disorder, he may appear sane on the witness stand. The key defense witness for my client was a psychiatrist.

Dovey, Jean, and I worked together on motions, trial strategy, legal issues, and jury selection. Among ourselves we were unguarded in what we said. We were protected by the most powerful and unassailable privilege known to the law—our right to defame the judge, the prosecutor, and the clients. In this case neither the judge nor the prosecutor inspired our defamatory skills. The judge was neutral, quiet, and decisive. The prosecutor had been an active criminal defense lawyer before he was appointed an assistant United States attorney. Once appointed, he closed the door on his defense counsel days. He was an aggressive but fair prosecutor. Jean and I knew him from his defense days. Dovey and he were good friends, but this did not deter him from pressing hard for a first-degree murder conviction.

The government built its case around an accomplice who had participated in the murder and who pled guilty to a lesser offense in order to get a break at the time of sentencing. The prosecutor surrounded the cooperating witness with corroboration at the key points. This did not deter Dovey and Jean. They raised legal issues, some strong, some weak.

Dovey's and Jean's styles were different. Dovey was not only a busy lawyer, she was a minister and a Sunday school teacher. She could get worked up against a witness who she thought, or others might think, was lying. Jean was calm, prepared, and relentless.

Jean went first in the cross-examination of the accomplice and Dovey exploited what Jean turned up. Dovey added righteous indignation. She wished to make it plain that this cooperating witness was someone who would say anything the prosecutor wanted.

She did this by getting the witness to give the first time he met with the prosecutor in order to tell the prosecutor the whole truth. Then the witness was asked to identify each of the eight successive meetings with the prosecutor to give the prosecutor a little more of the whole truth each time they met.

At the end of each trial day, we remained in the courtroom to review what had happened and how we would deal with the next day's witnesses. Despite the strength of the government's case and the fact that we were all tired out, we found a way to extract some humor and some optimism from the judicial process.

The testimony of an accomplice, a cooperating witness, gets special treatment from the law during the court's instruction. The court advised the jury that it should scrutinize the accomplice's testimony with great care before accepting it as true, and such testimony should be considered with more caution than the testimony of other witnesses. Our closing arguments exploited the court's instruction.

I still recall the prosecutor's rebuttal argument. It was good in all respects for the government and bad in all respects for our clients. Dovey whispered that the jury may bring in not only a guilty verdict but also a death penalty recommendation.

The jury did return a verdict of guilty as charged, but it reported that it could not reach a verdict concerning the death penalty. This shifted the issue to the judge. Dovey and Jean carried the day in urging the judge not to impose the death penalty.

For years after the trial, when the three of us happened to meet around the courthouse, the conversation eventually turned to the trial and Jean and Dovey's great "cross" and Dovey's great closing argument. I, of course, said a few words on my own behalf concerning my cross-examination of the government's psychiatric witness.

I have not seen or heard from either of them for many years. Dovey and Jean, if this note in a bottle reaches you up there or down here, please give me a call. You've got my number.

IRVING YOUNGER AND
JOE DiMAGGIO

T he recent TV program replaying the life and times of Joe DiMaggio brought to mind Irving Younger. Younger frequently worked into his continuing legal education lectures references to Joltin' Joe as the embodiment of perfection in his chosen work.

For those who may not know of Irving Younger, by common consent, he was the top banana on any CLE program. He brought the law of evidence to life with clever insights, humorous anecdotes, and inside stories. He extracted from the Federal Rules of Evidence a grand unifying theory that reconciles electromagnetism, gravity, and the speed of light.

His hearsay lecture was unforgettable, and his lecture on the art of cross-examination was even better. Each lecture was worked and reworked, so that anything that slowed it down was trimmed off. The final product had the impact of a fine vaudeville act. As he paced the platform, he took off his jacket and rolled up his sleeves. To emphasize a point he jumped into the air and screamed the applicable rule. When he completed his four-hour, non-stop lecture, he was the fighter who had gone fifteen rounds. He needed a robe thrown around him and the assistance of two handlers, one with ice water and the other with flattery.

He had excellent credentials. He attended Harvard under-graduate and the New York University Law School. He was an assistant United States attorney in Manhattan and thereafter was in private practice. He left private practice to serve as a trial judge in New York City. He then taught trial technique at Cornell, Columbia, Harvard, and Georgetown. In 1981 he joined Williams & Connelly. He left three years later to resume teaching.

In his lectures he reduced the technique of trying a lawsuit into ten black-letter rules. Learn them by heart. If you violate them, you do so at your client's peril.

He temporarily defrauded his audience of ambitious would-be trial lawyers into believing that each one of them was destined to be a prince of the forum, winning big cases, by following the Younger rules. It was while delivering his exhortations that he invoked Joe DiMaggio's memory and Joe's perfection in the New York Yankees' outfield and of course Joe's clutch hitting. Younger then shifted to the legendary triumphs of yesteryear's great trial lawyers. There was Max Steuer's cross-examination in the Triangle Shirtwaist Factory fire case. Steuer was defend-ing the factory owners charged with causing the death of factory employees who were unable to flee the burning building because the owners had locked the exits. Max Steuer's cross-examination consisted of asking the prosecution's key witness to repeat the story she gave on direct examination. She did so, word for word. That was the cross-examination. Thus, so Irving Younger proclaimed, Steuer demonstrated that the witness had memorized the story the prosecutor gave her.

He gave instances of what happens when the lawyer asks one question too many and converts a good cross-examination into a disaster. And he warned against getting too excited. There was the lawyer who got so excited in arguing an arson case that he exclaimed, "Ladies and Gentlemen, the chimney took fire; it poured out volumes of smoke. Volumes did I say? Whole encyclopedias, members of the jury."

He told of the lawyer who fainted dead away when appearing before Judge Learned Hand.

He preached elegance and relevance and brevity. No wasted motion, just like Joe DiMaggio. He was proud that a case he tried when he was a Williams & Connolly partner gave him the chance to perform like Joe DiMaggio.

Younger warned that the trying of cases requires a tolerance for disappointment. Trying cases is winning and losing. There was a lawyer in New York called "Last Chance Levy." He got his cases after the jury returned a guilty verdict. Levy was the postverdict and appellate man. He considered himself a winner each day the client was not behind bars. In one of his cases, the day came when all appeals ended and the defendant found himself in court for the last time. As he was being led away, he whispered to Levy, "What happens now?" Levy answered, "I shall be going to dinner and you are going to jail." Last Chance Levy developed a tolerance for defeat.

After several years in practice, Irving Younger returned to his real love, teaching trial practice. Although his life was cut short at age 55, he lives on by and through the videotapes of his great performances, recorded live before spellbound CLE audiences.

269

JOE NACRELLI'S
BAR REVIEW

Right after graduating from law school, I took Joe Nacrelli's bar review course. Nacrelli was a short muscular man in his fifties. He looked like he might have been a prizefighter in his youth. He charged $150 for the course. He said if you took his course and you attended class, he would give you good odds that you would pass.

On his bulletin board were letters from former students declaring that Joe Nacrelli made the difference. But for him they would have failed despite an Ivy League law school education. They were right. A significant number of Ivy Leaguers who did not take Nacrelli's course did not pass the bar exam the first time around.

Nacrelli gave each student an outline of the bar exam subjects and the previous three years' exam questions. He demonstrated to the class how his outlines provided the answers to the questions.

He was uninterested in grand legal theories. He was a master mechanic. If this (the facts), then that (the textbook rule of law), and don't waste time on something else. He told the class that they would have plenty of time for thinking about jurisprudential considerations when they are in their law office waiting for the phone to ring.

His English occasionally faltered, his pronunciation of legal terms was questionable, but that meant nothing. He knew bar exams and how to give the answer the bar examiners wanted.

In those days the bar examiners were senior members of the bar appointed by the judges of the U.S. District Court. Each had his own subject, year after year. He drafted the questions and graded his papers.

I had never met the bar examiners. They were remote, austere, and learned guardians of the gate.

Nacrelli psychoanalyzed each of them from a distance. He had studied their whims, their peculiarities, their obsessions, their misunderstandings of the law, and the type of answers they liked. For instance, I recall that Nacrelli said that Francis Hill, the examiner in wills and estates, was a stickler for defining the difference between a personal representative and an executor. No matter what the question, you must write a page describing the difference.

The bar exam kept to the traditional subjects such as real and personal property, evidence, civil procedure, domestic relations, contracts, wills and estates, criminal law and procedure, legal ethics, and constitutional law.

The week before the bar exam he gave the class of 300 a rousing pep talk. He had an 85 percent pass rate, and we were honor-bound to protect his average.

He said there were two ways to answer. Write everything you think you know about the subject raised by the question or write a short answer that hits the target. If you write a long answer, writing everything you think you know, you run the risk of demonstrating a broad ignorance of the law. If you aim for the target and miss, you have no backup position. Each student must make up his mind on this.

Many years later I was a bar examiner. What I recall most vividly from the experience was my fear of losing an exam paper. I never did, but I misplaced a few, and I could think of nothing else until I found them.

Before each exam the committee members exchanged the questions we had drafted. We decided that we should also pass around sample answers. Writing the questions was easier than writing the answers. We exposed to one another that we may be unable to answer our own questions.

One of the questions that came before the committee was what to do with an exam paper written entirely in Chinese except for some Latin expression such as res ipsa loquitur. When we looked at our rules, we discovered we did not state that the responses to the questions must be written in English. There was a discussion of this and then a member of our committee made a ruling. He said that since the questions were in English, an irrebuttable evidentiary presumption arose that the answers must be in English.

If Joe Nacrelli returned today, he would find that the bar review game is a big, lucrative business, a $50 million-a-year business dominated by several national companies. Rather than charging $150, as Nacrelli did, the bar review people of today are charging in the $2,000 range.

What is the future of the bar exam? Good arguments can be made that bar exams serve no worthwhile purpose, and if there is to be a bar exam, it should not be state by state. There should be one national bar exam. The practice of law has become national and so should the bar exam.

A client would not be competently served by a new admittee to the bar just because he passed the bar exam. The law has become too specialized for that.

There was a time when those gifted with a comprehensive knowledge of human behavior could pick up enough law to guide a businessman through a buy-and-sell agreement on Monday, try a civil suit on Wednesday, and work out a plea to a driving-while-drunk case on Friday. The days of the grand generalist are over.

JOHN MORTIMER

Horace Rumpole may be better known than John Mortimer, Rumpole's creator. Mortimer's legal career brought him to court in all kinds of litigation including the domestic relations practice he inherited from his father. He said his father extracted a living (even after he went blind) largely on the proceeds of adultery, cruelty, and willful neglect to provide reasonable maintenance.

Mortimer put to good use in his plays and novels the things he picked up in his law practice:

> I count myself extremely lucky to have been called to the bar in my twenties and to have immediately found middle-aged women, businessmen and suburban housewives ready to pour out all the secrets of their lives. I was fortunate enough to meet murderers, con men, contract killers, politicians with unrevealed scandals and, on one horrible occasion, an assistant hangman. All of this was a great privilege and seems

to me to have been more useful than moving, with the publication of my first novel—an event which happened shortly before I got called to the bar—into the world of editors, publishers and other writers. The bar exams are pretty dull, as is learning law academically when it's not connected with real human beings in trouble, but it's well worth it for the help you may get as a writer.

When Mortimer was active at the bar, he did not hold himself personally accountable for what was wrong with the profession. He took it as he found it. Mortimer did hold himself accountable for trying to be decent, which meant to him compassion, fairness, and, whenever possible, giving others the benefit of the doubt.

Rumpole is of the same mind. His encounters within the legal process bring him into scattered pockets of pretension and meanness (the opposite of decency), which Mortimer has Rumpole detect and deplore.

In Mortimer's most recent book, *Where There's a Will*, he writes in the first person as an 80-year-old veteran giving worldly advice that he knows will be of little use to those who read it. The style is that of his two earlier autobiographical books. He is prejudiced, ironic, opinionated, and skeptical. He adopts a self-deprecatory pose. I saw it in action when he gave a talk here in Washington. He opened by tapping the microphone and saying, "Can you hear me in the back row?" There were shouts, "We can hear you fine." Mortimer paused and said, "Sorry about that."

The book is a collection of short reflective essays covering many topics in addition to the law. Included is the recommendation to start the day with a glass of champagne and, if you are a writer, then write your daily 1,000 words right away.

In his chapter titled "Law or Justice," Mortimer criticizes a legal process that justifies cruelty under cover of declaring that the letter of the law must be enforced. Human problems sometimes get beyond the power of legal reasoning (whatever that is) to solve. He contends that the results of even the best laws, when consistently applied, are bound to be intolerable in many individual cases. He makes his point with a humorous story.

A client of his wanted a divorce (his wife also wanted the divorce) at a time in the 1940's when adultery was the only available grounds. Mortimer's client could not find someone willing to commit adultery with his wife. He devised a plan to solve the problem. He disguised himself with a false beard, false mustache, and dark glasses. In broad daylight, in front of the neighbors (the neighbors would be the witnesses), he entered his own house playing the part of the correspondent. He ended up in jail for corrupting the legal process. Mortimer's closing comment was: *What have things come to when a man goes to jail for joining his wife in bed?*

Mortimer demonstrates how a judge, by using a sensible trick shot, brings comfort out of contention:

> A judge who also had medical qualifications once told me the following story. He was trying, long ago, a perfectly friendly action between a woman's husband and her lover to determine which of them, and they were both well off, should pay for the child's education and fixture support. The parties agreed to a blood test and when the judge got the report it was perfectly clear that neither of the two men before him, but some third man, possibly a penniless stranger, must be

the father of the child. The judge tore up the report, threw it into the wastepaper basket and invited the two men to his room. There he told them that the blood test had established nothing with any clarity and that they should agree to share the cost of bringing up the child. What he did was certainly against the law and, just as certainly, right.

JUDGE BRYANT

Villiam B. Bryant rose to the top of his profession by virtue of his talent, character, and that necessary vitaminizing agent required for success, *la forza del destino.*

My memories of Judge Bryant go back to the late 1940's. He was one of those seeking to establish himself as a lawyer when no jobs were available to him despite his outstanding academic and military record.

He put together a frugal office arrangement of sorts on Fifth Street opposite the police court. This qualified him as a member of the Fifth Street irregulars, solo practitioners happily scratching out a living trying misdemeanor cases and occasionally springing someone in a felony case.

If we were to take a walk up Fifth Street on a spring morning in those days we would see the old and graying Columbian Building. Its tenants, solo practitioners or two-man partnerships, are on the sidewalk taking the sun on the Fifth Street Beach.

They are colorful individuals, cultivating their idiosyncrasies. Among them are bondsmen busily carrying on their economically rewarding, symbiotic relationship with the bar. Each bondsman is surrounded by his clientele, defendants to be walked to court for a 9:30 appearance. Most will plead guilty and, if their lawyer is in good form, they will escape with a fine.

The Fifth Street irregulars complete their working day around midafternoon. The rest of the day is given over to card games or an occasional trip to the racetrack. Bill Bryant spends his afternoon reading law in a friend's office and, when a distraction is needed, winning in nine-ball at the poolroom up the street.

Bill, or "W.B." as he was called by friends, did what many of us did. We showed up in the police court each morning hoping that the arraignment judge would assign us a case.

Here is the way it went. A defendant arrested the night before is brought before the court. The presiding judge asks if the defendant has a lawyer. If the defendant says no, the judge appoints a lawyer from those sitting on one of the front benches. The lawyer might or might not be paid a few dollars by the client.

The pay was unimportant. What was important was the hope that we could demonstrate some ability in the courtroom, win a few cases, and wait for established lawyers and bail bondsmen to refer paying cases to us.

Bill quickly became a winner. In those days the art of cross-examination was a thinking-on-your-feet, spontaneous art. There were few documents and no discovery. Bill sensed when a witness was not telling the truth. He exposed the lie and then stopped when he made his point.

His practice was varied. It connected him with informers, witnesses, police officers, and other types that defy a label. It contributed to his lifelong interest in what may be called the human experiment.

The prosecutor's office recognized Bill's ability and invited him to join the U.S. attorney's office. An assistant U.S. attorney is dressed in brief authority giving him power that he can use or abuse.

Bill followed *Berger* v. *United States*, 295 U.S. 78 (1935), which prescribes that a prosecutor must play fair. Getting a guilty verdict by striking foul blows to get that verdict is in itself an offense against our system of justice.

After his tour of duty as a prosecutor, he returned to private practice and reestablished himself as a leader of the criminal trial bar. Judges assigned him serious pro bono cases such as the capital case of *Mallory* v. *United States*, 354 U.S. 449 (1957). Bill took it all the way to the Supreme Court, which reversed the conviction and established the right of a criminal suspect to be brought before a judge promptly after arrest. All this kept Bill busy. He described himself as the busiest poor lawyer in Washington.

In 1965 President Lyndon B. Johnson appointed Bill to the United States District Court, where he distinguished himself for the next forty years, winning the respect of all, including defendants he had sent to jail.

Many unsought honors came his way. The most recent is the naming of the courthouse annex in his honor. Judge Bryant avoided the press. His philosophy was "Live by the press and you will die by the press."

When an aspiring judgeship applicant is asked in the crucial interview what judge he or she would use as a model, Judge Bryant's name frequently heads the list.

Judge Bryant had his professional disappointments, the most significant being the 1987 enactment of the Federal Sentencing Guidelines. His trips to the jail (both as a defense attorney and as a judge), and his extensive background as defense counsel and prosecutor, gave him a unique insight in determining what a fair sentence should be. The guidelines turn away this resource in favor of a cold, rigid calculation by preset numbers and, worse yet, put the prosecutor in control to determine the crimes to be charged, which in turn determines the sentence.

The result is we have the largest number of people of any civilized country passing through our jails. Changing the guidelines will not be easy. Parts of the prison system have been outsourced to private speculators who have an economic stake in preserving the guidelines.

W.B., wherever you are, when the guidelines go, as go they must, the Fifth Street irregulars shall raise a glass to you and recite an *encomium*.

JUSTICE

The Sunday paper carried the review of a new book titled *Outside the Law*. The book is a collection of essays concerning what that elusive word justice means in real life. Colman McCarthy wrote the review.

Mr. McCarthy is only an average student of what justice is. But he is an honor student when it comes to spotting injustice. He speaks on the subject in a rich Brooklyn accent in classes at Georgetown University Law Center and as a visiting lecturer at local high schools. In a sly, amiable way he intimidates his students with references to the lives and writings of those who have arraigned injustice. The combination of that folksy Brooklyn accent and the parables of the likes of Mahatma Gandhi and John Ruskin—with frequent Latin references—makes his lectures a unique experience.

As he speaks we learn he is a pacifist and a vegetarian. I saw Brian Lamb's interview of McCarthy on the C-SPAN program *Booknotes*. As McCarthy preached the vegetarian creed and the problem of cruelty to animals, Lamb cast a glance at McCarthy's well shined shoes. The glance was not ignored. McCarthy acknowledged that the shoes looked like leather but—with a twinkle in his eye—he told Lamb not to worry. The leather was fake.

McCarthy is not one who gets lost in abstract justice philosophy and books by John Rawls. He dives right in with indignation at the gratuitous injustice everywhere around us. He urges people not to deliver up injustice and to rectify the injustices of others.

He acts out anecdotes. He tells of the lawyer he met who is dealing with the injustice inflicted on Florida sugarcane workers. Reenacting the moment when he discovered the lawyer had an impressive academic background and could have signed on for big money, McCarthy goes into an ironic cross-examination of the lawyer.

"What is the matter with you? Were you disbarred or something? You were trained to go after the big bucks. What the hell are you doing down in Florida depriving the corporate raiders of your talent? Your family must be ashamed of you. Who are you trying to fool? I bet if I looked into your case I'd find that you're on the lam, and when things blow over you'll go back to Wall Street where you belong."

He then plays the lawyer's role. "I did all the things you suspected. I chased the big bucks but I didn't want to spend my life distributing injustice. I wanted to represent the victims." McCarthy gives additional examples of those who ended up going straight.

I attended a lecture in legal ethics McCarthy gave at American University's Washington College of Law. He asked the class to go out to Ward Circle and count the number of red cars and black cars that went around the circle in exactly five minutes. The students did so. When they returned to the classroom McCarthy asked those who had seen black cars and those who had seen red cars to raise their hands. The students raised their hands. Then he turned on them. "Why did you do that damn fool thing I asked you to do? Here you are, law students—supposed to be of a critical state of mind—and you follow my nonsensical direction. Now you know why it is so easy for a dictator to start a war."

With this as the introduction, he gave his spoken essay on nonviolence. The delivery was different from what one would expect from such a lecture. It was filled with humor, wisecracks, amusement at his own spontaneous ingenuity, and cascades of casual knowledge. He was all prepared for such questions as, How does nonviolence work with a person like Adolf Hitler? His theme was that Hitler was not dropped by parachute. The bad boys gain power step by step and, for those with eyes to see, the pattern of injustice is visible at the early stages. That is where to stop it.

McCarthy could broaden his knowledge concerning injustice if he were to practice law for a few years. Every busy lawyer has felt its stab. There is nothing like it. It alters the blood pressure. It causes rage. It stays with you. And I speak only of injustice directed toward a client.

I have discussed with lawyer friends how they present a case where the client has been the victim of an injustice. Should the advocate make a strong dramatic appeal? Should the advocate demand that the injustice be corrected forthwith? There seems to be agreement that, no matter how harsh the injustice, a dramatic demand for prompt retribution against the wrongdoer generally does not work. Judges are wary of such appeals. They have heard too many. Jurors may be caught up in a dramatic appeal but it is only temporary. Juries are a composite. I have heard it said that the poetic types give way to the accountant types as the deliberations continue day after day. The emotional appeal has no staying power.

The injustice we see in the practice of law comes in many forms. There is the articulate liar who prevails over the inarticulate victim. There is the just cause that gets strangled by a manufactured complexity. There is due process extended beyond human endurance. There is the bully determined to ruin lives to justify some neurotic concept of law enforcement. There is always on display what Justice Robert Jackson identified as the most odious form of oppression, the oppression wearing the mask of justice.

LEROY NESBITT

On November 24, 1998, I
saw that I would see no more. Leroy Nesbitt's name was on the
obituary page.

Leroy was zealous in pressing his client's case, but his zeal
carried no tinge of meanness. Everything about Leroy was—as
the saying goes these days—transparent.

When we met by chance there were three things we talked
about. First was a lawyer that Leroy and I knew well. This lawyer
had lived a full life and had explored the *terra incognita* of all the
world's pleasures. Leroy and I gossiped about the close calls such
explorations produce.

Second, we spoke of a client that I had a brush with and
Leroy had represented. The client placed Leroy in a difficult
position, and it took time and work for Leroy to disassemble the
frame that the client had tried to put around Leroy. During it
all Leroy was his usual cheerful self. It is what one endures in a
demanding trial practice.

The third topic of conversation was the 1972 mass conspiracy trial where Leroy's talents were on display for many
months in the United States District Court. There were fourteen
defendants, and each defendant was represented by a star of the
criminal bar and each determined to show off to the full extent
of the law. The government used as its key witness to prove the
elaborate conspiracy a man who bore the unfortunate last name
of Crook. Imagine the opportunities this opened up.

During the trial Leroy held his own. He jabbed like Sugar
Ray. He blocked like Rocky Graziano. He skepticized like William Buckley. He was cool like Atticus Finch, and he delivered a
knockout punch like Ali. Leroy's client walked.

Leroy's days were spent in the criminal courts either in
trial or awaiting trial. As the English barristers say, Leroy did
criminal. As a criminal lawyer he had to accept the big minus of
such a practice—unless he got paid up front he was unlikely to
be paid posttrial. He knew the rules. If there is a guilty verdict,
the lawyer is to blame. If there is an acquittal, the government
didn't have a case.

But the minus must be weighed against the positive com-
pensating balances of the criminal practice. There is the cama-
raderie. The goodwill that exists among comrades at the bar.
Lawyers representing co-defendants enter into a formal joint
defense agreement. This confers a privilege with respect to
disclosures among counsel in preparing the joint defense. The
unwritten element in such defense agreements is the obligation of defense counsel to remain cheerful and to participate in
the gallows humor that accompanies the criminal practice. The
humor often turns on the implausibility of the defense in the
face of the government's evidence. The humor may involve the

idiosyncrasies of the trial judge, the prosecutor's desire to protect his reputation by bringing a 32-count indictment where each count is based on the identical facts. The humor may turn on the need to keep the defendant off the witness stand despite his belief that he can acquit himself with a good story. Or that his mother is a credible alibi witness. Or that he discovered in the very jail cell where he is confined another person who will corroborate the alibi defense.

Then there are the things to be learned from people who have gotten themselves in trouble. One learns that a defendant who appears to be evil through and through is, if one wishes to be honest about it, a person suffering from a mental disorder. Perhaps he should be put away, but that does not prove that his plight is entirely explainable in terms of free will. Human nature rarely appears in absolutes. W. Somerset Maugham put it this way:

> There is not much to choose between men. They are a hotchpotch of greatness and littleness, of virtue and vice, of nobility and baseness. Some have more strength of character, or more opportunity, and so in one direction or another give their instincts freer play, but potentially they are the same. For my part I do not think I am any better or any worse than most people, but I know that, if I set down every action in my life and every thought that has crossed my mind the world would consider me a monster of depravity.

The goings-on at the courthouse itself are additional protections against taking ourselves too seriously. The delays. The misunderstandings. The surprise endings. The incompetence of the competent and the preposterousness of the self-important.

All part of the human comedy so well described by Balzac and Dickens.

The *Washington Post* obituary reported that Leroy was mentioned frequently for appointment to the bench. Leroy would have made a reasonably good judge. I never saw him doze off during a discussion of cases on all fours. And he had energy. And he certainly knew the front and back of the judicial system. But I doubt that he would have enjoyed judging as much as he did lawyering. He was fitted for what he did—to test his work product against an adversary. He also had a unique advantage. He was one of the few with the discipline required to concentrate on the documents related to his next trial while awaiting the jury verdict in the case he just tried and in which he gave his all. Try it sometime.

LET'S AGREE TO DISAGREE

> How I hate the man who talks about the "brute creation,"
> with an ugly emphasis on brute. ... As for me, I am proud
> of my close kinship with other animals. I take a jealous
> pride in my Simian ancestry. I like to think that I was once
> a magnificent hairy fellow living in the trees, and that my
> frame has come down through geological time via sea jelly
> and worms and Amphioxus, Fish, Dinosaurs, and Apes.
> Who would exchange these for the pallid couple in the
> Garden of Eden?
>
> W.N.P. Barbellion

Why is it that people are
so resourceful in finding ways to disagree? Why do we devote
so much time to contention and bickering? I used to have these
thoughts as I walked up the steps to the courthouse carrying a
briefcase stuffed with pleadings asserting claims, counterclaims,
third-party claims, and cross-claims.

Then one happy day I came across Clarence Day's *This Simian World*. It gave me the answer to my questions. The edition
that first came to hand contained a preface by Dean Acheson. Mr.

Acheson said that his copy of *This Simian World* was given to him by Oliver Wendell Holmes Jr. Justice Holmes recommended it as helpful in understanding the human condition.

Clarence Day begins his book by recalling a conversation between him and his chauffeur. They were out driving one Sunday afternoon along upper Broadway in New York City. The chauffeur was put off by the swarm of disagreeable people aimlessly strolling up and down Broadway, all chattering away at one another. Didn't people have something better to do than argue with each other?

Clarence Day remarked that groups of people aimlessly moving around and arguing is distinctively simian. We should feel no disappointment at seeing something that is inevitable. We are descended from apelike or monkeyish beings. We are not lions and tigers or eagles, solitary and uncommunicative. Lions and tigers and eagles have a majesty and dignity that chattering, squeaking, chirping, quarreling simians do not have. Solitary felines would not have descendants like lawyers "spending their span of life on this mysterious earth studying the long dusty records of dead and gone quarrels. We simians naturally admire a profession full of wrangle and chatter but that is a monkeyish way of deciding disputes, not a feline." Whatever a simian does, there always must be some chattering, chirping, and quarreling about it. Simians cannot even make peace without a kind of chatter called a peace conference.

After I considered what Clarence Day had written, I understood why Justice Holmes and Dean Acheson found *This Simian World* a significant book. Now when I watch the PBS National Geographic programs showing the carryings-on of ape-like, monkeyish animals, I see things in an altogether new light. I see that the simian days follow a pattern I can understand. They get up at six in the morning. They scramble around for the next two hours in search of food. After breakfast they take a short nap. When they awaken, well rested, they form groups and begin to mill around, nagging each other, stealing and hiding food, attacking and retreating, giving the appearance of rage and indignation, and all the time chattering, chattering, chattering. This is the part of the day that simians devote to litigation. It goes on for two hours before the afternoon recess when it is nap time again.

The point of it all is that we, as simian descendants, should see litigation as self-realization and we should enjoy it. It is the very essence of us.

The simian's compulsive bickering explains the proliferation of procedural rules. We have federal rules, circuit rules, local rules, and each individual judge's rules, and best of all, we have the abomination euphemistically titled the sentencing guidelines.

Our simian litigiousness require lots of rules of engagement. That is why it is so difficult to repeal rules. It takes more energy and discipline than we are willing to give it, and when we try to do something about it, we give the job to a committee. A committee repeals no rules. The best it can do is write the rules to be used in determining which rules should be considered for amendment, or rewriting, or repeal.

I now understand why *Williston on Contracts* runs twenty volumes or more. *Williston on Contracts* is not what I once thought it was—the rules of contractual agreement. It is in reality a study of the ways in which people use the rules to disagree.

Does the concept of the contract—you do this and I will do that—connect with our simian ancestors? My speculation is that it does. I mentioned earlier that the simians, after the afternoon nap, organize themselves into groups. These groups collect around a leader. Each leader patrols the territory in search of unattached simians to add to his group. As a leader approaches an unattached, the chattering commences between them. What is this chatter all about? My speculation is that the chatter is a negotiation of promises. The leader says join my group and you will be part of the most powerful group. The unattached says I will join your group on condition that you treat me right and protect me and my food from others. A promise for a promise.

LOUIE'S

The need to inflate a résumé in order to meet the competition tempts me to include in my own résumé the words *connected with the FBI*. That statement, when read quickly, could mislead the reader to believe that I at one time was an FBI agent—an impressive credential, almost as good as saying I was a Golden Gloves boxing champion.

If pressed to explain those words connected with the FBI, I would submit that I went to the same high school as J. Edgar Hoover, Central High, located at 13th and Clifton streets, N.W. But more important, I would add that I bought my clothes at Louie's, where Hoover and all the FBI agents bought theirs.

Louie's was located a few blocks west of the courthouse on the north side of D Street between Sixth and Seventh. Louie was Louie Goldstein. He specialized in good conservative men's suits of a style a little to the left of Brooks Brothers and J. Press. He sold for less because his suits were factory seconds, suits with an insignificant manufacturing defect. It might be the repair of a torn lining or a misweave in the cloth. Louie was quick to point out the defect.

Louie did his work in rolled-up shirtsleeves with a tape measure around his neck and a piece of tailor's chalk in his upper shirt pocket to be used to mark up the cuffs (take up or let down), the waist (take in or let out), and the pants (give a short break). Louie quickly calculated a customer's size just by looking. "You look like a 39 regular. Come over to this rack, and we will see what we have in your size."

J. Edgar Hoover insisted on well-dressed agents. He was a young man when he found his way to Louie's, as many young lawyers did. After he became director and he could get clothes anywhere he wished, he stayed loyal to Louie's. He referred the agents to Louie, who put them in the FBI uniform, either a dark grey flannel or a dark worsted single-breasted two-button suit.

Louie's became the lawyer's clothing store of choice for a number of reasons in addition to J. Edgar Hoover's recommendation. Louie's was near the courts and the Fifth Street office buildings where solo practitioners and two- or three-man partnerships had their offices.

If, when Louie announced the price to a young lawyer, he detected pain in the lawyer's expression, Louie would put ten dollars in the pants pocket of the suit when he delivered it.

When someone would say to Louie, "There is no label in the suit. Who made it?" Louie's answer was, "This is a Hart Schaffner suit. Marx wouldn't have anything to do with it." Louie then said, "Look here. If you want labels, you should go up to Fred Pelzman's high-class, high-rent store on F Street. You'll get a label and you will pay double. Don't tell Fred I said that."

There was another men's clothing store on D Street that sold new and used clothing. It was named simply Best Clothes. The proprietor stood in front of the store looking for people who were looking for Louie's. He could spot them right away and he would invite them into his store. If a customer asked if this was Louie's, he would say "Louie's West."

Louie knew what was going on. He had customers who were lawyers at the Federal Trade Commission, located close by at Sixth and Pennsylvania Avenue. He enjoyed taking an FTC lawyer outside on the sidewalk and pointing out Best Clothes' unfair and deceptive trade practices going on within three blocks of the FTC.

"Isn't there something called the Sherman Act that makes what you see going on here a criminal offense? Why don't you guys put a stop to it?" The FTC never opened an investigation of this clear Sherman Act violation.

The Gayety Burlesk Theatre was located at Ninth and F streets. The burlesque comedians did a sketch that was a knockoff of the Best Clothes operation. The scene was a men's clothing store. The customer was played by a burlesque comic. The salesman was played by the straight man. The salesman puts a suit on the customer. The suit is too big, too small, too long, and too short. Each time the customer complains, the salesman corrects the problem by pinning it up or pulling it down, or putting in some stuffing. When the salesman completes his work, the customer is bent over and can hardly walk. The customer steps out of the store onto the sidewalk. A passerby says to another, "Look how well dressed that poor crippled fellow is."

I took a walk last week along D Street between Sixth and Seventh to see how it compares with its 1950s golden age.

Everything is changed. New buildings on both sides of the street are of no particular character. The six small shops that were there are gone. The men on D Street are not dressed like 1950's FBI agents. If Louie were here, he would feel compelled to mark the sleeves (take them up an inch) and the waist (let it out three inches). It takes a real prodding of the memory to identify the spot where Louie's was. I think I located it, and I put on the front of the new building occupying the space where Louie's was a mental plaque bearing the words *Louie's—Good Suits for Good Lawyers.*

When I see an old-timer at a bar dinner, I ask if the tux he is wearing came from Louie's. He looks on the inside of the jacket and reports there is no label, so it must have come from Louie's, followed by the proud statement, "This tux must be fifty years old."

THE MYSTERY MAN

I n the department of ... perhaps, it
is better not to name the department. It will be better for us to
designate the department in question as a certain department. In
that certain department there was a certain official, an Inspector
General, who had no background as a prosecutor or investigator.
He had no political connections with prominent personages. He
was neither a lawyer nor an accountant. He had no cell phone.
He saw no need to have two press agents.

A week after his appointment, he met with his staff. He
asked each to introduce him- or herself and give a background
sketch. Each had substantial experience in criminal prosecutions
and investigations.

When the introductions were concluded, this mystery man
(that is what his employees called him behind his back) said his
appointment came to him as a surprise. All he knew was he had
a six-month job and, thereafter, he would return from whence he
came. He opened with this:

I am trimming the budget. The budget is much too large. Cutting it back will keep us from investigating defenseless people who violate meaningless regulations. Is there not a RAND study declaring that we have more criminal laws, regulations, and rules than any government in the history of the world? The more laws, the more offenders, the more work, the bigger the budget. The laws that are required are suffocated by those that are needless.

With all these rules an Inspector General with a big budget could easily pin a violation on just about anybody, innocent or guilty.

We'll use our spare time to do some reading on the job. Let's start with Nikolai Gogol's short story, *The Overcoat,* and his play, *The Government Inspector.* After that we will read Herman Wouk's *The Caine Mutiny.* Better yet, let's get the movie and watch Humphrey Bogart playing Captain Queeg. We will discuss this at our next meeting.

Do not try and figure out my political interests and then do something that you think a person with my political interest would like done. I understand that people with a prosecutorial or investigatory bent often spend time investigating their co-workers. I can save you some time. I'm investigating myself.

The staff did not know what to make of their new Inspector General. However, when they looked over their case files, they found that two-thirds of their cases were make-work projects, inquiring into other people's personal lives.

The real cases, the cases that required careful study, wisdom, insight, proportionality, and, heaven forbid, compassion, were sitting on the window sills.

After the first monthly meeting, work went smoothly. The staff nipped in the bud Ponzi schemes, pyramid schemes, and other significant bad acts.

The mystery man opened the second monthly meeting by announcing that one of the staff had resigned. Unknown to the mystery man, this person, who had the praiseworthy custom of attacking those who cannot bite back, was in communication with his brother-in-law, a prominent personage. This person informed the prominent personage about what the Inspector General was doing, especially reducing the budget. The prominent personage advised his informant to resign so he would not be tainted. At the proper time, the present Inspector General would be exposed and removed to make way for the informant.

The Inspector General said he would like someone on the staff to find the author of these quotations:

> … the least thing is seen as the center of a network of relationships that the investigator cannot restrain himself from following, multiplying the details, so that his descriptions and digressions become infinite. Whatever the starting point, the matter in hand spreads out and out, encompassing ever vaster horizons, and if it were permitted to go further and further in every direction, it would end by embracing the entire universe.

★★★

> … guilt and crimes are so frequent in the world that all of them cannot be punished. Many times they happen

301

in such a manner that it is not of much consequence to
the public whether they are punished or not.

The Inspector General opened the third monthly meeting
with these words: "I see we have completed eight cases that were
over a year old. You know I like this job. I like giving orders. I
must confess I like power. I am beginning to see why everybody
else likes it."

As his last month approached, the people in the office
decided to present an award to the Inspector General. What
could they give him? He did not collect things. He lived alone.
His interests were his work and his reading.

While the committee was in the process of meeting with
the Inspector General concerning an award, two men appeared
in the office. They said they were there on important business.
They wished to be alone with the Inspector General. They closed
the door and were with the Inspector General for ten minutes.
When the door opened, the Inspector General said he must
attend to important matters with these two men. He did not
know when he would be back.

He never did come back. The people in the Inspector General's office learned two weeks later that he had been returned to
the mental institution from which he escaped six months earlier.

ROY THOMPSON, SENATOR GORE, MOMAN PRUIETT, AND GORE VIDAL

I f you happen to see in a used bookstore a copy of *Moman Pruiett: Criminal Lawyer*, buy it. My copy disappeared in 1945. I did not see a copy again until Roy Thompson found me the copy that is before me as I write. Moman Pruiett was an Oklahoman "who defended 343 persons charged with murder. The record shows 303 acquittals and the only client to hear the death sentence pronounced was saved by presidential clemency." That is a record that should be of interest to every lawyer.

Roy Thompson is a well-known local lawyer of great distinction. When, in a conversation with Roy, I learned his family history had commenced in Oklahoma I asked whether he had ever heard of Moman Pruiett. Roy quickly asked me, "How did you hear of Moman Pruiett?" I told him I had read Pruiett's autobiography. Roy then filled me in on a few things. Roy's father came from Oklahoma to Washington in 1907 to work for Oklahoma's first senator, Thomas P. Gore. Years later Roy

Thompson himself went to work for Senator Gore. When Roy became a member of the D.C. Bar, he developed a law practice that included the representing of Oklahoma Native Americans.

And now the Senator Gore-Moman Pruiett connection. Senator Gore, in 1913, opposed lawyers who were pressing a claim for large legal fees against the Chickasaws and Choctaws. When Senator Gore could not be bought off, the lawyers decided to frame him by setting up an accusation of attempted rape. The accuser was Minnie Bond. The perpetrators went to the United States Attorney in the District of Columbia and asked that Senator Gore be arraigned on a charge of attempted rape. The U.S. attorney refused. How could he get a conviction of a blind senator on a charge of attempted rape? Minnie Bond's handlers did not give up. Minnie sued Senator Gore in Oklahoma for the attempted rape and added a count for defamation of character.

Senator Gore employed as his counsel the leader of the Oklahoma bar, Moman Pruiett. Pruiett, in his autobiography, gives his closing argument in defense of Senator Gore.

Here are samples:

In the box where you sit, Gentlemen of the Jury, you have an unusual advantage over my friend and client, the defendant. You can see him but he cannot see you. He is in the dark. He cannot look into your faces and judge from your countenances what manner of men you are, whether you are his friends or his enemies— whether you are all good men and true, or whether any or all of you may not be prejudiced against him by the false tale told you by the lying lips of a vile woman and her still viler co-conspirators and confederates. He has had to depend upon me and upon my judgment concerning all and every one of you.

This worries me exceedingly. He tells me that he relies upon me implicitly to put his case truthfully and fairly before you in my argument. This also troubles me—for how can he rely confidently upon another man whose face he has never seen?

There is another thing that stands in my way. My client is versatile and scholarly and has a profound knowledge gained from the many books which his wife has read to him and shown to the eyes of his mind.

On the other hand, I, his adviser and advocate, am unlettered and without the knowledge of books, for the only book I have studied is the book of human nature. From that book, and that alone, I do believe that I have learned how to judge correctly of a man's actions by his motives, and, conversely, to discover his underlying motives by considering carefully what he has done. From that book of human nature and a habit of long observation, I have grown to believe that I can very often read correctly the thoughts and emotions of men with whom I become acquainted and whose faces I can see, as I have seen yours for many days. But no man can always interpret correctly the thoughts of others by their faces, nor can a man always speak the proper words to his brother.

And I do believe that when a man is called upon to defend and protect the innocent by the words of his mouth, and he tries earnestly to do so, that help may and does frequently come to him from unknown sources, which enables him to speak effectively—to speak plainly, to call things by their right names, to denounce falsehood and conspiracy, and to protect the innocent and the upright from the assaults of all the liars and the pimps and the prostitutes who are still outside of hell.

Within seven minutes the jury returned its Not Guilty verdict. A contemporary newspaper story described Moman Pruiett's effort as follows:

Probably the man who has profited most from the Gore case is the man who cared least about profiting. Moman Pruiett, one of the senator's attorneys, won a lasting place in the hearts of every Gore sympathizer throughout the country by his burning castigation of the men behind the plaintiff. ... There is no gentility to Pruiett's eloquence. Even his sarcasm is blunt and ragged; it has no razor edge. He simply strips a proposition naked and he dresses it with homely, striking word pictures, or peppers it with trip-hammer blows of wilting invective. Naturally, he is deeply loved, desperately hated, and profoundly respected. And above all else, he is immensely interesting.

If your interest has been triggered, you can follow the subject in Gore Vidal's autobiography, Palimpsest. You will learn that the blind senator was Gore Vidal's grandfather.

LAW BOOKS,
CLARENCE DAY, AND
ARTHUR KOESTLER

We were talking about overhead. I said law books take up too much expensive office space. I emphasized the point by saying there are more law books on narrow tax issues than there are medical books about something really important such as the anatomy of the human brain.

He said he is glad there are more tax law books than there are medical books about the human brain. We already know enough about how our brain works to know we need all the law books we can get. He directed me to Arthur Koestler's comments on the human brain, where I found this quote by Paul MacLean, a distinguished expert on the human anatomy:

Man finds himself in the predicament that Nature has endowed him essentially with three brains which, despite great differences in structure, must function together and communicate with one another. The oldest of these brains is basically reptilian. The second has been inherited from the lower mammals, and the

307

third is a late mammalian development, which ... has
made man peculiarly man. Speaking allegorically of
these three brains within a brain, we might imagine
that when the psychiatrist bids the patient to lie on
the couch, he is asking him to stretch out alongside a
horse and a crocodile.

Arthur Koestler (1905–1983) said that the wild horse and
the cunning crocodile frequently outvote the reasonably prudent
man, two to one. And given the proliferation of atom bombs,
they may outvote us into the war to end all wars and all people.

Before the 1945 atom bomb explosions, each of us lived with
the prospect of his own individual death. But since 1945 we have
lived with the prospect of the death of the entire human race.

Koestler said a dispassionate observer, looking in from
another planet, would be astonished at our compulsion to kill
each other:

The most persistent sound which reverberates through
man's history is the beating of war drums. Tribal wars,
religious wars, civil wars, dynastic wars, national wars,
revolutionary wars, colonial wars, wars of conquest and
of liberation, wars to prevent and to end all wars, follow
each other in a chain of compulsive repetitiveness.

This bad brain of ours likes to give fanatical devotion to
the likes of Hitler and Stalin, who bring death to millions who
die for a dynasty, a religious belief, a political ideology. The individual crimes that fill the pages of the Metro section of the daily
paper—the thefts, the assaults, and the murders—are insignificant in number when compared to the world wars.

Koestler says we need a new drug, a mental penicillin to control the bad parts of the brain. Koestler did not mention mankind's only remedy, the law. It is undramatic, but it is all we have. The more law books the better.

Let me tell you more about Arthur Koestler. Romanian born, he attended college in Austria. He then got employment as a journalist, and he joined the Communist Party of Germany in 1931.

In 1937 he covered the Spanish Civil War and was captured by Franco, threatened with death, and imprisoned for ninety-five days. He obtained a release and joined the French Foreign Legion. Thereafter he found his way to England. In 1940 he joined the British army and made England his home.

By 1938 he had already seen too much of Communism, his God that Failed. Friends of his in the Communist Party had disappeared and others were fearful of their lives, not from those outside and hostile to the party, but from those inside the party.

Koestler exposed and condemned the party with his novel *Darkness at Noon.*

In 1998 a distinguished panel of writers ranked Darkness at Noon as the eighth-best novel of the century. It has been published in thirrty languages and remains in print. It is the story of a true believer in a Communist utopia who, during the 1930s Stalin purge trials, first confesses crimes he never committed in obedience to party loyalty and then denies them and ends a ruined man.

Koestler picked up specialized subjects as easily as he picked up languages (he wrote in Hungarian, German, Spanish, and English). Among Koestler's many writings is an article on humor. The trouble with the article is that Koestler had no sense of humor.

THERE WERE GIANTS
IN THE LAND

T he narrator in the novel I am reading commences this way: "Stupidity is not my strong suit." These words immediately brought to mind Frederick Bernays Wiener (1906–1996) and Judge Gerhard Gesell (1910–1993).

I start with Fritz Wiener. I recall seeing him at Connecticut and L in front of the Stoneleigh Court Building (no longer there), a beautiful antique apartment house converted into an office building. Although I did not know who Fritz was, I knew he must be somebody. He wore a cowboy hat that conflicted with his otherwise conservative dress. He sported mustachios approaching the style of Oliver Wendell Holmes Jr.

Sometime later I was introduced to him by a friend with whom I was taking a walk along Connecticut Avenue. "There is Fritz. I want to say hello to the Colonel." We approached Fritz and my friend introduced me. Pleasant words were exchanged. We resumed our walk. I asked who Fritz Wiener was. "Fritz is the leader of the appellate bar. He was in the

311

solicitor general's office. He also is the authority on military law."

Months later I called Fritz to ask him to take the appeal of a criminal case I had lost. Fritz suggested I come by his Stoneleigh Court office to discuss the case. Fritz had a working fireplace, large library rooms, and comfortable leather chairs. He lit up a cigar and analyzed the facts five different ways, reciting as he went along the relevant precedents.

Fritz was a grandnephew of Sigmund Freud. He graduated cum laude from Brown University and magna cum laude from Harvard Law School. He was assistant to the solicitor general from 1945 to 1948, when he entered private practice.

Fritz described in his book Effective Advocacy his favorite case, *Reid v. Covert*, 354 U.S. 1 (1957). In that case the Supreme Court first ruled against Fritz. He moved for reconsideration. Granted. Yes, granted. He reargued the case. The Supreme Court reversed itself.

Fritz, in 1972, had a victory before the Supreme Court in a case involving the rights of a private club. He was then retained to file the petition for certiorari in another case with similar issues. He had every reason to believe the petition would be granted. It was denied. The only justice who voted to grant certiorari was a justice for whom Fritz had a minimum of high regard.

Fritz took this very hard. He said that things had reached the point where it was time to call it quits. Doris and he had decided to say goodbye to the law practice and settle in Phoenix, Arizona. Perhaps the cowboy hat he wore reflected his desire to wind up way out west.

Before he left, his friends convened a going-away party at the Army and Navy Club. In attendance to wish Fritz and Doris goodbye were a group of well-wishers that included judges and lawyers who knew Fritz at every stage of his career. The evening came off very well, with Fritz's friends telling stories of Fritz's star performances before the Supreme Court. There were descriptions of Fritz in his swallowtail coat, the only remaining private practitioner who dressed in such formality.

A friend recalled that in one of his appearances Justice Felix Frankfurter commented to Fritz, "Mr. Wiener, you are speaking of the conduct of the prosecutor at the trial level. Let me say that when I was a prosecutor in the Southern District of New York we would not think of doing such a thing that you describe." Fritz's reply: "Justice Frankfurter, there were giants in the land in those days."

Another friend recalled Fritz's definition of a perfectionist. He is a person (Fritz) who takes infinite pains himself and gives infinite pain to others.

Now Judge Gesell. His father was a distinguished child development specialist connected with the Yale faculty. Judge Gesell was Yale 1932 and Yale 1935. He commenced his legal career as adviser to the Securities and Exchange Commission chairman, William O. Douglas. In 1941 he joined Covington & Burling's trial section, specializing in antitrust and major corporate litigation. He had served on a number of presidential committees, including the chairmanship of the President's Committee on Equal Opportunity in the Armed Services, 1961–64. In 1967 he joined the United States District Court for the District of Columbia.

Judge Gesell was of medium height, portly, with a florid face topped by a full head of white hair. He had a dramatic, authoritative speaking voice. He could be irreverent. He could be gruff. He could be friendly. He could be contrarian. He could be all four within five minutes.

His grasp of the facts and law was intuitive and instant. As a trial progressed he knew where the lawyers would go if he let them. He curbed them by saying, "Sir, some lawyers—of course you are not one of them—might be tempted to ask questions that would be out of place in a case like this. I know you will not do that."

Judge Gesell, decisive by nature, recalled an SEC commissioner who could not make up his mind about anything. "If I met him on a staircase, I could not tell whether he was going up or coming down."

He took few things under advisement. Whenever the issue was close, he used oral argument to decide which lawyer was in the right. He listened first to the lawyer requesting a ruling. When that lawyer began to falter, Judge Gesell stopped him right there and asked the other lawyer to comment on what was just said. A few minutes of this give-and-take and Judge Gesell had what he needed to decide the case.

He believed that practicing law involved going to court and speaking up. He did not want the court to just become a document warehouse.

WHO WAS HE?

When Phineas Indritz died, the papers described him as a distinguished Washington lawyer who served as legal counsel to several congressional committees. They described his accomplishments as an advocate who participated in some twenty-five litigated cases and the drafting of fourteen statutes, all aimed at bringing to an end discrimination based on race or gender.

The obituary notices, although reasonably good in describing Indritz's legal career, omitted what I found most interesting in my acquaintanceship with him. He had, as my wife pointed out, all the distinguishing characteristics of the mild-mannered Clark Kent, better known as Superman. In a social setting Phineas was invisible. His style was the absence of style right down to his clip-on bow tie. Try to describe what he was wearing and you could not. Try to engage him in conversation concerning who he was and what he was up to and you learned very little. He turned the conversation away from himself in the Clark Kent style.

Later you might learn that this invisible man defended the
helpless and fought injustice and succeeded where others failed.
In addition, you would learn he was an exceptional athlete with
the Olympic acrobatic skills of a circus performer. On a personal level, I discovered that he brought to excellence a number of things I wanted to do but lacked the required talent to
accomplish.

I give a few examples. I am, at best, only a fair juggler,
despite years of practice. Finny was a great juggler of balls, hoops,
clubs, and cigar boxes. I learned to do a handstand only after
years of practice. Finny did handstand tricks on the high parallel
bars. I have seen a picture of him as a young man doing his one-
hander on the rim of a downtown Chicago water fountain.

As a juggler Finny was a showoff. As a lawyer he was invisible. He worked behind the scenes and remained unseen unless
he appeared for an oral argument. His specialty was what matters
most—the conversion of unjust laws into laws that protect people
from injustice. He identified statutes that caused real harm, albeit
under the authority of the law. Then, by changing a few words
of a statute, he reversed it so that it worked against the mean-
spirited.

I had the honor of working on a few cases with Finny.
He was indefatigable and imperturbable. Nothing an opposing
lawyer said or did, and nothing a judge said or did, disturbed his
equanimity. It was only when things went well that he became
apprehensive at the unreality of it all. His cases involved issues
that generated strong feelings and hot tempers. But not for Finny.
He had emotional intelligence of a high order.

I never met or even heard of anybody else who had Phineas's
array of talents. And let me add another of his talents. He was a

great teacher. As inept as I am as a juggler, Finny taught me how to toss and receive juggling clubs with Finny as a partner. Only a great teacher could do that.

Finny preserved his remarkable and restless curiosity all his life. Every year he called and reminded me of the annual jugglers convention, a convention he attended in search of new juggling tricks.

Up to the very end he responded to calls from members of Congress to assist in the drafting of curative legislation. He was a proofreader's proofreader.

Finny had the Benjamin Franklin gift—a common-sense ingenuity about everyday things. Twenty years ago we were together on a bar association trip to the Caribbean. I was standing with him to retrieve luggage in the airport. As the conveyor belt came around, there appeared a piece of luggage covered with white polka dot splotches. Finny took it down. I asked him what accident accounted for all the white paint. He said he splashed it on deliberately so he could easily identify his among all the other luggage. If one day you happen to see luggage splotched with white polka dots coming around on the conveyor belt, it is mine.

LaVergne, TN USA
14 December 2010
208755LV00001B/2/P